DISRUPTIVE
LEADERSHIP

Eight Counterintuitive Secrets for
Running a Successful Business

Chris Catranis

D1245720

Leaders
Press

PRAISE FOR DISRUPTIVE LEADERSHIP

The author captivates you immediately and does not let go of you. You won't be able to put this book down. I would categorize this book as a JOURNEY, not just information. Emotionally I've never felt so good after reading a "leadership" book. They just don't get written like this one.

On the other hand, the real-life examples and techniques are simple yet effective. If you start reading this in the evening you will not be able to wait for work the next day.

Get this book for yourself, a member of your tribe, a family member. It is a MUST read.

– Mark Nureddine |
CEO, Bull Outdoor Products and
bestselling author of *Pocket Mentor*

I thought I had read every leadership book worth reading on the planet. Wow. What a wonderful surprise! I found this book to be unique, inspirational, and easy to read. There are so many great tools and ideas. One of the top books I've read for business knowledge and techniques. HIGHLY RECOMMEND.

– Joe Dinoffer |
President, OnCourt OffCourt

A powerful theme threads throughout this entire book. It's how you treat people that matters more than anything. Words of encouragement and truly showing your team you care creates raving fans out of employees. Words of shame and scrutiny leave scars that can never be overcome.

It takes work to do things from a standpoint of positivity. It's easy to be harsh and negative. But it is worth it to adopt a culture that is unwavering in the way people are cared for in the organization.

We have an opportunity as leaders to have an impact that can ripple out to the families and friends of our teams. Read this book. It will give you the blueprint!

– Ali Razi |
Founder & CEO, Banc Certified Merchant Services

How many books are there on leadership? There will be tons more, and many will have potentially lasting effects on the reader. Don't fall into the trap of thinking that everything has already been said. This book proves that wrong. Treat yourself to an amazing experience and BUY THIS BOOK.

Whether you are new in business, have leadership experience, or have decades of seasoning in your chosen craft, this book will make a difference. You can also apply the strategies and concepts to volunteering, parenting, the list goes on. If you get this book you'll read it more than once. I know I did!

– David Fuess |
CEO Catapult Systems and
bestselling author of *Why They Buy*

Having experienced working in toxic environments, this author has shown me clearly why those organizations let that happen and what I can do to make sure it never happens again. If every manager and C-level executive read this book and applied the concepts, all companies would be fun and productive!

It has been a long time since I have been so inspired by a book, especially yet another leadership book. There are many out there, but you will NOT regret getting this one.

Note: *****Make sure you have a pen and note-taking materials ready. There is so much good information and practical, ready-to-implement-now advice that you will want to make a swipe file to refer to.

– Rick Orford |
Co-Founder of the Surplus Academy and bestselling author
of *The Financially Independent Millennial*

It is a fact that if you "follow the herd" you get mediocre results. There are many books on leadership, so you might ask yourself why read another? This is NOT your typical leadership book, because it clearly shows you through the author's stories and examples how his contrarian views and methods have created amazing results for his personal life, business ventures, employees, and partners.

Chris Catranis is entertaining and a wildly enjoyable storyteller. You will not be able to put this book down and will take valuable nuggets from it into your life. Read it and don't forget the popcorn!

– Allen Sanders |
Financial Strategist and Founder of Empowerment Concepts

Leaders
Press

ISBN 978-1-943386-46-8 (pbk)
ISBN 978-1-943386-45-1 (ebook)

Library of Congress Control Number: 2019939054

Do you want to partner with Chris?

Go to www.chriscatranis.com
and find out how you can get involved in
Chris's next project!

DEDICATION

I dedicate this book to my wife of 42 years, Beth Ann, who has been with me through all the disruptive events of my adult life, including the birth of our ten children.

ABOUT THE AUTHOR

Chris Catranis is an experienced entrepreneur who has devoted his life to bringing technological progress to remote areas of the world. He has participated in bringing disruptive innovations to international markets for more than three decades.

In 1978, he graduated from Syracuse University with a degree in international trade and export marketing. Chris began his career in international trade and finance, founding a domestic international sales corporation, USABROAD, Inc., with warehousing, customs clearing, freight forwarding, wholesaling, barter trade, timbering, satellite telecommunications and civil engineering operations in Africa, Asia and Europe. In 1995, Chris returned to the U.S. to found Skyway Partners, the first in the U.S. triple-play building local exchange carrier (BLEC) network.

From 2001 to 2003, Chris owned and operated Subscriber Networks, an early application service provider for property owners of multiple dwelling units that operated their voice, video and data networks.

Since the beginning of the Iraq war in 2003, Chris has lived in the Middle East. He was the first U.S. civilian businessman on the ground in Iraq, when he went in search of a new business venture in 2003. Within a short period, he had formed Babylon Telecommunications, Inc. (Babtel), a company which won an AAFES contract to build a managed IP network on one of the busiest airports in the world and one of the largest U.S. military installations in Iraq. Chris managed that network and 16 similar networks until the withdrawal of U.S. troops in 2011. Chris spent most of 2012-2014 working independently as a consultant for several companies in Afghanistan. During that time, he also developed a menu of new commercial applications for cloud-based network services. Chris currently remains a COO of Babtel while splitting his time 50/50 between Qatar and the U.S.

INTRODUCTION

I've always had fun, and I've always made money. I've lost money too, but I've had fun doing that as well. I don't know if that's considered success or not — but if that's success, I'll take it.

Throughout this book, I will show you a disruptive leader's path by telling you a series of true stories that you may be inclined to doubt. I urge you not to do so; because not only did they happen as I describe, but they shaped me into the person I am today. Why is this important? Because it was in following the eight principles of business that I'm going to share with you that enlightenment, success and change was able to happen for me and everyone I associate with in business endeavors.

I didn't learn these principles until I was locked up in a Lebanese prison a bit later in life. I heard a voice say, "Clean the toilet," and that's when things changed for me. It wasn't a guard or an inmate who instructed me to do so, but a voice from elsewhere. Stay with me here; I didn't understand it at the time, nor do I claim to understand it now. From that point on, everything started to become clear to me. I now look for the 'toilet' to clean every day, and good things happen. Of course, it's not quite that simple, but I'll lead you down that path in the following chapters.

Given my rather unorthodox life experience, if I can adapt these eight principles that I'm going to share with you to create a successful business path, anyone can. There have been plenty of books written to advise others on how to succeed in the traditional workplace. Few of them, however, address how to lead or inspire others in what we could call the unpopular or the less prestigious positions. While cleaning the toilet may not top your list of ideal tasks, there's no denying that it must be done.

All the stories you will read illustrate how enthusiastically engaging others in a common goal with grace and compassion leads to success. If that's considered disruptive, so be it. No matter who you are, or what you do in life, you will find something of value in the space between the front and back covers of this book. Incidentally, this space I reference is just about the same distance as the space that will one day be between the birth and death date on your tombstone. It's what happens in this space that matters as each person's story will lead to the same lessons and revelations once taken apart and examined.

Years ago, I watched a movie about outer space with one of my daughters. As a 9-year-old, she was astounded by the movie's depiction of the wonders of the universe. After the film ended, since it was a clear night, I suggested we go outside and look at the night sky. When you look at the stars with somebody you love, there's not much you can say that's more moving than the power above. No matter what you attempt to articulate, it'll fall flat like a pebble hitting the bottom of an empty bucket. Nothing matters but that vast landscape above and all around you.

I asked my daughter what she saw above her, and she answered, "Stars. Many, many stars."

I asked, "What else?"

"Planets and planets, all over the place."

"What else do you see?"

She wrinkled her nose, gazing above, "Well, I think I see some airplanes."

"But what else?" I persisted.

The conversation went along this way as she described all the things she could see. She was, however, too young to understand what she could not see. As she listed all the things floating around in space, she never mentioned space itself. Finally, I asked, "Well, what about the space?" and she laughed at the obvious answer to what was all around her, but she hadn't been looking at the sky in that way.

A challenge in life for many is we forget about the space because we are drilled into the planets and stars and airplanes. Space is what offers the potential for creation, change and growth. All the opinions going around are subject to change; they don't matter all that much. What does matter is what's not changeable — and one thing that doesn't change is the truth. The permanent things in this life are essential. If it's mutable, it's not going to be around forever, and so it doesn't matter that much. That nonetheless is where we tend to put our focus. I'm going to ask you to remember the space.

How this philosophy matters as it pertains to the instruction I'm going to layout and the stories I'm going to share is that what lasts forever is your mark on the world. You determine your legacy in your behavior and interaction with other people on this planet — every day and in every moment. If you treat every human interaction as a sacred event, that's a success; that's a legacy worth leaving.

Another point I'm going to make is that time is irrelevant in examining our human experiences — in other words, it's never too late. If you've failed at a particular moment, you can succeed in the next one. We all fail, and we all succeed. The secret is recognizing that both experiences are crucial to success.

I'm going to remind you that life conspires to help you in everything you do; life itself is a conspiracy to assist you in every way possible. The forces of the universe conspire to help you live a fruitful life that benefits others. We can help each other win. It doesn't matter if it's in business or writing or relationships. We can have a wonderful life experience.

As you learn the eight principles in this book, you might not draw the same conclusions I did, but I promise that you will put this book down having changed in some way. I know it's a bold assertion, but I stand behind it. Putting these eight principles in practice will help you grow further into the person you're meant to become. My goal is for the practical application of these points to come through in such a way that you can easily apply them to your own life.

To conclude this introduction, I must mention the disclaimer that success and failure are two ends of the same sausage. If you're going to play this game we call life, you're going to eat the whole sausage — both ends of it — and that means you're going to experience failure and success. You may as well make good friends with that fact so you don't get emotionally charged by either outcome; you can't get puffed up when you succeed or feel brokenhearted when you fail.

Failure is an inherent and inevitable part of success. It would be best to learn to enjoy failure just as much as success because both will come and both will go. If you can't be happy with failure, success is never going to be enough for you. Living a bold and disruptive life means you will both succeed and fail multiple times. That's how you learn, and how you grow. Mistakes and failures are the ultimate teachers that will lead you to success in career, family, friendships or daily interactions with others. In my companies, we know that failure happens and I'm going to illustrate how we handle it professionally with our team. Our company's ethos centers around the idea that what you do with failure is what counts.

When I ask people to invest in my companies, I tell them the mission is more important than making money. How's that for a disruptive ask? I urge potential investors to keep the purpose in mind as being in alignment with the target is how they make money. Focusing on the success or the dollar signs and expecting that the method I employ will work can't be a part of the process.

After many years in business, I read Heather Plett's blog post, "What it Means to 'Hold Space' for People, Plus Eight Tips on How to Do It Well," (https://heatherplett.com/2015/03/hold-space/ accessed on March 6, 2019). Her instruction was a life-changer for me, as it laid the groundwork for my company's principles. It enabled me to put together a cohesive body of ideas that I could articulate for my people and which now form the eight value points of my business. While I've spent a lot longer than four years learning these principles in theory, it was when I read the writer's post that it all came together for me. I'm very much indebted to her for articulating what I already knew and paving the way for me to work with both my people and my customers using these principles. Now I wish to pass this knowledge along to you.

I work each of the eight points into all my contracts with customers and personnel as these points form the basis for my philosophy on how I run my organization. I'll take you through each concept one by one in of the following eight chapters. I admit that it's often tricky for people to embrace these principles because it's counterintuitive to run a company the way that I do. Rather than firing people, or punishing them for their failures, I wholeheartedly encourage trial and error. Every person on our team must make mistakes to learn valuable lessons, and I greatly value their path. Why would I throw any of them out and start the whole process anew with somebody else?

The values that I hold dear and that have been so well articulated by Heather Plett are woven into our contractual agreements and our relationships with customers and anyone with whom we deal. Each chapter of this book is based on the exploration of one of the following tenets.

❖ Permit people to trust their own intuition and wisdom.

❖ Give people only as much information as they can handle.

❖ Don't take their power away. When we take decision-making power out of people's hands, we leave them feeling useless and incompetent.

❖ Keep your own ego out of it.

❖ Make them feel safe enough to fail.

❖ Give guidance and help with humility and thoughtfulness.

❖ Create a container for complex emotions, such as fear and trauma.

❖ Allow people to make different decisions and to have experiences that are different from what you would expect.

Has this path I will set out worked perfectly every time? I'll let you be the judge. Sometimes it's all in the way that you look at it. The color of life depends on what color glasses you wear as you look back. I have the habit or character trait that when I look back, I turn everything, no matter what it is, into a happy story and something beautiful.

Recently, I asked one of my teammates, "Do you think I'm a success?

"What's a success?" he asked.

"Perhaps it's somebody who makes a lot of money and never fails," I offered.

He laughed, and said, "Chris, you live your whole life with two principles: have fun and make money. That's a success. It doesn't matter if you make money or lose money."

Fortunately, using the tenets I'm going to describe, I've made more money than I've lost. I've also had a lot of fun along the way and maintained many relationships with my team, customers and investors, which can be a tricky road to run. I do my best to make life better for the people who cross my path. I've made amends to the people I've hurt. I've made much money for people. Most importantly, however, I strive in the hope that when my life is over, I'll be able to say that I left the world a better place than I found it.

If that's the definition of success, I'll take it.

CHAPTER ONE

PERMIT PEOPLE TO TRUST THEIR OWN INTUITION AND WISDOM.

Permit people to trust their own intuition and wisdom. In the course of our work, we all run into situations where we have no prior experience to rely on, and yet, intuitively, most of us know what to do. We encourage our people to trust their own intuition and the accumulated wisdom from the many years our people have been working together.

Often, I see that the people who appear to be successful are motivated by fear. They're accustomed to being told, "Do what I say, or you're going to get fired." That's not how I operate, nor is it how we treat our people at my companies. I pride myself on saying I'm the worst employee in the company, and everybody laughs, but it's true. There's only room for one worst, and that's me. How this pertains to how we treat our teams is that rather than motivating them by the fear of being punished or fired, we encourage them to trust our collective intuition and wisdom.

Success in life is primarily determined by how you handle what crosses your path. Every single human experience you have as an encounter with another is a sacred event, including the store clerk that you greet at the corner store. If you don't handle your interactions sacredly, you'll see people as just salespeople or customers instead of human beings. The cruelest thing we can do to a person is to reduce them to a concept of any kind, such as an employee or a boss. This terminology weakens our interactions.

Say you're walking down the street and an elderly woman asks you, "Excuse me, do you happen to know where 57th Street is?" You don't know, so you could blow her off and tell her you have no idea or to ask somebody who knows. Alternatively, you could walk her to the doorman of the next building, and ask him which way is 57th Street. In that case, you went out of your way, and that's good, but how much nicer would it be if you walked her to 57th Street? How many people will go the extra mile?

That's a divine opportunity; a sacred event to be of service that you can experience nearly every single day. All you have to do is open your eyes to the possibility of others, and your life will change. Life brings these opportunities to you, and we often ignore them; we let them pass. Perhaps you've forgotten that every human being is incredibly valuable. Pay attention to that human who is interacting with you in some way. Listen and care about them; it's not hard to do. You might struggle to find a way to help someone, but that doesn't mean you can't listen and at least think about it.

If I had to categorize my style of business management, I'd say my philosophy lies somewhere between the entrepreneurial

American and the Danish form of management in which an employer hires a person to do a job and says, "Go for it. Let me know if you need help. Otherwise, I'm out of it." I like to fuse those two styles with elements of the love and kindness reflected in the teachings of the Buddha and those of Jesus. Integrated with this style of management is allowing others the grace to trust their intuition and wisdom.

My path to this management style started when I was 7 years old at a small barber shop in a little suburb outside of Buffalo, New York. As I waited for my turn in the barber's chair, I read through the latest *Hulk* magazine, and an advertisement on the back page listing a submarine for $15 caught my little eye. The ad touted all the bells and whistles that a boy would think a submarine would have. It read, "Imagine going under the water in your submarine and firing torpedoes!" The marketing was clever, and the writer made the sub sound like it was real.

Well, $15 was a lot of money back then. I got so excited about the submarine, however, that I told all my friends at school about how I was going to buy a sub for $15. Naturally, they got fired up about it too, and soon they were begging me to get in on it. I asked how much they could put in, and they offered about 20 cents or their lunch money for the week, and in no time at all, I'd collected $5.

Then my father came along and asked what I was up to. He was a technology entrepreneur and an engineer, so he was quite curious about my budding business. I told him that I was buying a submarine and showed him the article that I'd torn from the *Hulk* magazine. I excitedly listed all the benefits of owning a sub, including how I was going to go through Lake Erie and that I would be cautious not to go over the falls. The more I talked about it, the more excited I was about the idea of the submarine.

My father asked, "Is there any way I can get in on the deal? How much more money do you need?"

When I told him I only had $5, he asked if he could put up the remaining $10.

I said, "Well, sure you can, Dad."

"But I want extra rides."

"I don't even know if you can get in the submarine, Dad," I said. "I think it might be made for kids."

He told me we would work something out, but he was sure he could get in it. "If it's a submarine, they're going to make it big enough for a man, don't you think?"

I agreed with him and took the $10 and sent away for the submarine. For the next ten days, I was the most excited guy in the world as I waited for my delivery. Well, ten days came and went, and when my submarine finally showed up at the house, it was just a piece of cardboard you could set up in your room and imagine you were floating around.

I felt like the biggest jackass in the world.

My father came home from work and asked, "What's the matter, son?" I started crying and showed him the cardboard and said, "This is the submarine, Dad."

"Well, that's a disappointment, isn't it?" he said. "What did you learn?"

"I learned I'm probably the biggest jerk in the world to think I could get a submarine for $15," I said.

My dad looked at me and said, "No, son. You've learned something much more important. You might not know what it is right now, but you will someday."

I didn't know what he meant by those words, but I figured it out later. With all the ideas I would have during my career, one worry I never had was about raising capital; I never gave a thought to the success of my endeavor. I got excited about an idea and shared it with other people, and they too got excited and wanted to be a part of whatever I was excited about.

My father allowed me to learn a powerful lesson by letting me trust my intuition. He could have thrown a wet blanket over the whole idea and explained that the submarine was not going to be real at that price point. He could have told me that real subs would not be advertised for sale in the *Hulk* magazine and that even if they were, they would cost $1 million. At the very worst, he could have laughed at my idea.

How, though, would that reality and cynicism have affected my young mind? Certainly not in a positive way. Instead, my father permitted me to dream, to imagine, and to get excited about the possibility and potential of one of my ideas. The important part was not that the submarine was misrepresented and that I blew $15, but that I had great enthusiasm to inspire others to act. It felt like being a superhero.

Unfortunately, my father had a severe stroke when I was 14, and he never recovered. He was an entrepreneur before his illness, and I greatly missed his guidance when I no longer had it. Dad's advice would, however, become quite clear to me a bit later in life after I graduated from college and began my first business.

I started my entrepreneurial career as a bookman (a seller of encyclopedias) when I was 17 by lying and saying I was 18. At that point, I was a high-school dropout. Although it was legal for me to work, I wasn't supposed to be driving at night until I was 18, nor was I supposed to be signing contracts. I read an ad seeking people to conduct interviews in Syracuse, New York, where I lived. The announcement made the company sound like they were an educational survey company and I was eager to get behind that gig.

My mom drove me to the interview, where we joined about 30 other people to listen to the speaker describe an incredible sales opportunity. Most of the others got up in the middle of the presentation and walked out; they were smart enough to know that it was a con job to get us to sell encyclopedias. I was, however, sucked right in.

I listened to the woman as she described the need for people to expand their worldview and live their lives as self-starters. Everything she said was beyond alluring to me, as her speech was designed to make people feel like important individuals destined to be something in this world. I was already a big fan of Napoleon Hill's *Think and Grow Rich*, so her style was appealing to me. She'd been trained by one of the top automobile salesmen in the United States at the time.

This sales pitch was designed to put together teams of door-to-door encyclopedia salespeople. Mostly it was a mill where they'd entice 20 or 30 people to come in and listen to a shpiel in which they tried to make the opportunity sound like it was for a consumer-survey company. Once you were in there, they put the pressure on to make you believe you were going to be participating in something beyond your wildest expectations and dreams.

Because I was just 17, I was quite gullible and bought right into the sales pitch. My mother stayed for the interview and listened, but she shook her head from side to side like it was a ridiculous idea. Like my father, however, my mother didn't try to steer me away from my intuition. It didn't go over all that well when the woman who did the presentation interviewed me, and she did everything she could to get rid of me.

First, she said, "I don't think this is for you. I don't think this is going to be something that you will want to do."

"I want to try," I assured her.

Next, she said, "Well, it's probably not something you're going to succeed in."

"Well, how do you know?" I asked. "If I don't try, we'll never know."

Exasperated, she finally said, "Well, if you insist, then give it a try. I guess I'm not going to say 'No'."

Thus began my career in encyclopedia sales. I believe I got roped into the idea because I was a fan of *Think and Grow Rich*.

In particular, I loved his quote, "Whatever the mind of man can conceive and believe, it can achieve." That was the whole idea behind his think-and-grow-rich mentality. As far as encyclopedia sales went, I conceived and believed, and set my sights next on achieving.

Out of the 30 people who were initially in the room that night, perhaps ten of us stayed. Only six of us made it through training because you had to memorize the whole pitch. We were taught to go up to the prospect's door and knock. When somebody answered the door, depending on whether it was a woman or a man, I asked, "Are you the lady of the house?" or "Are you the man of the house?"

I was told they would ask, "Are you selling something?"

"No, no. I'm interviewing people in the neighborhood to see if they're interested in education and how they feel about education in this town. Do you have a couple of minutes?" I was to say as I walked right in.

I was told they would then usually say, "Oh, go ahead and sit. Can I get you some coffee?" I would get some favorable attention because they thought I was involved in a project to improve the educational system.

When I first started the gig, it was so difficult to get in the door. I hit doors for two weeks before I got in one. I only got in three doors that whole month, and in one of the houses I got in, they called the police on me after I disqualified them. They told the police, "Some kid is trying to sell us encyclopedias, and he did his pitch so bad that he disqualified us because we didn't want to buy the books!" They said they wanted the police to get me off the street because I was causing trouble, so I was arrested.

In the meantime, all the other guys were selling books. I don't know what was wrong with me, but I had a feeling deep down inside that I was getting conned yet I wanted to be duped, and I wanted to con other people to see if I could do it. It was more of a contest with myself to see if I could pull off the nonsense. I was determined to succeed, as I figured that was how you made it in the world: convince and pressure people to buy stuff so you can make money. (Yeah, I know I was off track, but that's the point of this chapter.) I probably stayed at the job a lot longer than the average guy before it occurred to me that I was doing something that wasn't helpful to me or anybody else. In the beginning, however, I just wanted to see if I could do it.

A few of my fellow salespeople sold sets on their first night in the field, or at least within three or four nights, as we had learned an effective pitch. It took me a while to develop the skill to push the idea across to people and get them locked into the pitch. After a month or so, I still hadn't sold a single book. At 30 nights out and 100 doors a night that had to be 3,000 doors I hit. Undeterred by my stint in jail, I kept going out every night, and then finally I struck gold. I hit the third door of the night, walked in, did my qualifier, rattled off my pitch, sold some encyclopedias, and walked out of there with a check for $600. As that was more than 40 years ago, it was a lot of money.

After 30 days of completely blanking every single night and people trying to get rid of me and telling me there was no possible way I was going to succeed, I sold a set. After I sold that first set, I went to the next house and sold another set right next door. I kept working that block, and when I got to the end of the block, I sold another set. I hit my first triple by selling three sets in one night after 30 days of not getting in a dozen doors.

Finally, I had my pitch down. After I got in the door, I said, "Let me introduce myself. My name's Chris Catranis, and I represent the special promotional staff of Grolier Interstate." Many people knew that Grolier Interstate made the *World Book* and *Book of Knowledge* encyclopedias, but when they brought that up, I said, "Oh, yes, we do make those books, but we are the world's largest producers of mouse traps and water skis. Are you familiar with us?"

They said, "Oh, I didn't know you made mouse traps."

Now, I don't think Grolier ever made mouse traps or water skis, but that was the best way to deflect them. Next, I said, "So the reason I'm here is that I understand that this particular community has many people who are educationally minded. And Grolier Interstate has come out with some new products, and we'd like to find out if families are interested. I've got the capability tonight of providing three of these promotional packages to this community. We are, however, only looking for qualified families who, if we were to leave these products with them, would want them. The only reason I'm here is to find out if you're one of those families."

I gave them the idea that they had to sell me, and it wasn't me selling them anything. When asked about the cost, I said, "Well, if you think it's going to take the food off your table or the roof from the house, of course, you don't qualify under those conditions." I had some beautiful, glossy foldouts that I'd take out and throw on the floor. The images were beautiful, and people would fall all over themselves to have those books. I'd demonstrate how well made the books were by grabbing a page in the middle of the book. I'd shake that page in front of them and say, "These books are made to last forever." Well, I hardly had to sell after that.

The whole time I was in their home I was qualifying them by asking questions such as, "Are you sure you're the kind of family that would take advantage of this set if you had it? Would this be something you could see yourself reading to your children and helping them succeed with their school work?"

"Oh, yes, we would!" they'd say.

Sometimes people would catch me in the middle of my pitch and say, "Get the hell out of here! I'm not going to buy this bullshit! You're just selling encyclopedias." That happened a lot at the beginning, but it hardly ever happened after I learned how to sell. I drilled into the frequency of getting people to qualify themselves for me so that they could have one of those special promotional packages. I was emitting that in everything that I thought and did, and they hardly ever asked me if I was selling anything at the end because they were too busy qualifying themselves.

After my initial successes, I hardly even had to talk. I would walk inside and throw the glossy photos down on the floor and say, "Look, this is a special promotional offer. You can either have it or not have it. I don't have much time for you. However, if you show me that you're interested in this, I'll leave it with you. However, you have to be legit. Do you have any change in your pocket right now?"

They'd answer, "Oh, I have about a buck."

I'd say, "Well, let's say you pay 60 cents a day and you can make payments, and that's all there is to it. You can support our efforts to get out there and promote these great products." My pitch was ten minutes long, and there was no crap about it. I got right in and got right to the point. Half the time, they'd cancel the check before I even got back to the office — however, half the time they didn't. I did this for a little more than a year and earned the distinction of selling the most triples in the Northeastern United States during that period.

Then I became a crew manager and a field trainer, and by the end of that year, I was teaching other people to sell. I started out making $60 a set; then I went to $90 when I became a crew manager, and got a crew to manage. When I started training people how to sell, they paid me $120 for each set I sold. I got an override on everybody under me, plus $120 per set out of $600 for my sales. That was a ton of money for a teenaged kid.

The problem was that to get people to produce, I was told to take my crew out every night and get them drunk. At 10 p.m., we'd all come back to the office and then head out for drinks. Then every Saturday I had to take them to the race-track and pretend like I was making three times as much money as I did, inspiring my crew to produce and be like me.

Eventually, I concluded that was not what I wanted to do with my life. I learned that people could be convinced into doing almost anything. I could walk down the street and knock on doors and convince people to buy something that they didn't want, and they didn't need, and not only did I get paid for it but I made a lot of money. The minimum wage was less than $2 an hour, and I made probably $600 a week selling encyclo-pedias door to door.

Everybody in the business was drunk or prone to some sub-stance abuse, as they led rough lives. At first, I thought that bookman life was the greatest thing in the world. As it went on, I realized that that was not what I wanted to do. I won-dered why I was selling books for somebody else. Why didn't I work for myself instead? That year I heard a motivational tape about a guy who started an insurance company and was giving a talk to the million-dollar round-table salespeople. One of the guys said, "We make plenty of money as insurance salesman as we are selling life insurance. What makes you so special?"

He said, "When you sell premium, you only get 10 percent. When I sell premium, it's 100 percent my money."

I realized that if you start a company and build your busi-ness, you're not working on commission anymore; you get all the money that comes in and have control over the whole thing. By then, I was 18, and had been a bookman for about a year, so even though I was a high-school dropout, I still had a chance to finish. I went back to high school and asked if I could return. They agreed to give me one more chance but they told me that if I screwed up again, I wasn't coming back.

So I went back to high school in upstate New York that September at 18 years old, and at first I had a hard time adjusting to being a high-school student again. Then, in November, my mother died of a heart attack. The stroke disabled my father, and suddenly the pressure was all on me to support my dad, my sister and my brother. I was in a park in upstate New York when a young man walked up to me and asked if anybody had ever told me about Jesus Christ.

"I went to Sunday School my whole life," I said. "Of course, I've heard of Jesus Christ."

He said, "No, I mean Jesus Christ of the Bible." Then he witnessed to me and said that if I could pray the sinner's prayer and repent from being a sinner and accept Jesus into my heart, he would change me and make me a new creation and forgive me for anything I'd done wrong.

That sounded to me like a fantastic deal to me. My mom was dead; my father was very sick. I felt like a complete loser as I'd ripped off all those people selling encyclopedias and was trying to finish high school. If I trusted in Jesus Christ, I could be forgiven entirely and start all over. It sounded good to me, so I said, "Count me in. I want to start over again. I want to be reborn. Let's do whatever we have to do."

He said, "Okay. Well, let's pray the sinner's prayer."

We prayed the sinner's prayer, and I didn't feel any different, so I asked, "What do we do now? What's next?"

He said, "Now you start the long process of what's called sanctification. Little by little, you leave your old life behind, and your new life starts. However, it takes time, and you have to reprogram yourself completely."

I agreed to go with him to prayer meetings and Bible studies. When I got into the prayer group, I found a beautiful, giving, generous spirit among the people who were there that I'd never experienced before. They were the kind of people that I wanted to become, so I started to spend a great deal of time with the prayer group.

After my mom died, we were living on my father's Social Security to the tune of $240 a month. The older women in the prayer group realized what a mess my life was. They saw that I was trying to take care of my family going to high school during the day and working at a gas station on the minimum wage during the night. I took any job I could get to supplement the family income, including working at the ski slope nearby.

The women in the prayer group got together and said, "This is a hardworking kid. Maybe there's some way we can help him." Together, they came up with a great idea. One of the women's husbands was the head of the metric conversion division at Carrier, an air-conditioner manufacturer, in Syracuse. He had authority over people who were hired and being relocated. Because of his position in that catbird seat, he knew all the houses that were going to be cleaned and purchased and readied for the new people moving in. He agreed to take me on to clean the carpets, so I rented a carpet cleaner.

Because of his position at Carrier, I knew all the empty homes that would need to have their carpets cleaned, so I was able to gear up for it and be ready to roll on a dime. I hired people to clean the carpets for me; I didn't do it myself. That was how I started on the road to redemption as a carpet cleaner for the Carrier Corporation. By the end of my last year of high school, I'd made more than $20,000 cleaning carpets.

During my last year in high school, I had an excellent English literature teacher, and she knew I was a fundamentalist, so she introduced me to the writings of Thomas Aquinas, Jonathan Edwards and C.S. Lewis. Those tremendous Christian minds completely changed the way I saw the world unfolding in front of me as a young man. I became more and more intensely committed to praying and fasting. The teacher who was helping me get my Christian perspective in line would ask me things like "What do you want to do? What do you want to go to college for?"

By the end of the year, I decided I wanted to go into the Foreign Service. I couldn't get into college because I hadn't taken the SATs, so my teacher talked to the dean of the Maxwell School at Syracuse University and told him about me.

He said, "Send him over. We have a special grant program for kids who are dropouts or drug addicts or in jail. We have a scholarship for guys who are complete losers. He sounds like he might qualify."

So I interviewed, and they said something along the lines of "You win. You're the biggest loser we've ever met."

I was given the scholarship to go to the Maxwell School at Syracuse in their undergraduate division to study international relations. I changed my major to international trade and export marketing — a combination of the School of Management and the School of Public Policy. How I ended up with the degree I have and on the course I'm on was all due to my high-school teacher. All along the way of my life, special people would meet me at different intersections when I least expected it, and I would receive unexpected help.

When I went on to college, I continued my carpet-cleaning business as a college kid working my way through college. I went to people's doors as I'd learned to do with the encyclopedias, but this time I told them the truth. I would say, "Ma'am, I'm going to Syracuse University, but I'm paying for it by cleaning people's floors. I have my own steam-cleaning business. Would it be okay if I came in and gave you a quote? There's no requirement to buy. I want to tell you what we could do for you." No matter how many doors I went to, I got into every single one, and each time I went into one of those doors, I sold at least one room.

I had a hard-working crew who did the actual cleaning, while I was the manager of the business. I made my own soap to save money, which amounted to about 50 percent in savings; I bought the ingredients and mixed the soap myself. I did my best to try and figure out ways to get more profit out of the business, and we made $50,000 a year on carpet-cleaning jobs during my college years.

Then I got a job at Syracuse University as the coordinator for business, law and government internships. I'd an office and a secretary, and since the position paid $30 an hour, I didn't have to do anything else and was able to focus on my school work. I finished college in three years with a 3.98 GPA (cum laude). I came out of college without going into any debt at Syracuse, which was one of the most expensive schools in the country. At the time, it cost $20,000 a semester, but I paid my way through.

During my last year of college, a family walked into church that I recognized from the time I worked at the ski slope when my dad got sick after my mother had died. They were a family of skiers with four girls — all beautiful — and two boys. One of the daughters, Beth, had been 12 or 13 when I saw her on the slopes. As I watched the whole family skiing together, I thought, "What a beautiful family. If I do anything in my life, I want a family that goes out skiing together on Saturdays." The mother and father were both on the ski patrol, and all seven kids were skiing. I recognized they were so different from my family. My family was sick with strokes and heart attacks, and I wanted to live a healthy life and raise a family that had fun together.

At church that day, I saw that the girls had grown up, as it had been a few years since I'd seen them. I was drawn to Beth, but since she was 15 and I was 19, I thought that that was probably too big an age gap. I decided to wait until she was 16, and in the meantime, I worked my way into the household. I got myself invited over to dinner, and then I kept visiting. I brought gifts for Beth's mother and family that I paid for with my carpet-cleaning money.

When Beth turned 16, I asked her to go out with me.

When we went out together, I told her, "Ever since I saw you for the first time when you were a little girl, and I saw your family, I wanted to be a part of your family, and I think I wanted to marry you."

She said, "You're out of your mind!"

"I don't know if I'm out of my mind or not, but I feel strongly attracted to you and your entire family," I said.

"You're a little bit nuts!" she laughed.

I said, "I'm probably a lot nuts."

She put up with me, though, and nine months later, we were married, and she turned 17 on our honeymoon. I put her through college, and I got my undergraduate degree in international trade and export marketing because I wanted to create an export trading company.

After I graduated, I couldn't get a job in my field. As I left a meeting in downtown Syracuse, in that same office building, I saw a listing for a company called Sales Associates. Just for the heck of it, I walked in and said, "I have some sales experience. I'm graduating from college, and I don't have a job. Do you have any jobs?"

They asked, "Do you have any insurance experience?"

"I'm a million-dollar round-table insurance salesman," I said. "I'm the internship coordinator for business, law and government internships at Syracuse. One of the internships that I set up was at Northwestern where I became an insurance agent for them and was a million-dollar round-table member this year."

They set me up with an interview at Liberty Mutual Insurance Company, which was a great company, and they hired me right out of college. They gave me a $9,000 a year salary to start, and put me on the street. Compared to selling encyclopedias door to door, selling commercial, property and casualty insurance was like selling candy to a baby. All I had to do was save people money and deliver a good product, and they bought. That's how I started the next phase of my life selling property and casualty insurance for Liberty Mutual. It sounds like a boring story, and it is, but I did become the top salesman at Liberty Mutual within a year.

I sold mostly new, small accounts that were pizza, sub shops and liquor stores all over the southern part of New York State. Most of the small accounts paid around $7,000 a year in premiums for retail insurance. In the pizza and the sub-shop business in which they do a lot of frying, most of the fires start in the vent systems. I learned that if you could get somebody to make a vent-cleaning contract, you'd get a 20 percent deduction reduction of the rates in New York State on the fire rates. I started a vent-cleaning contracting company through a friend who didn't have a job.

I used all those contracts in my submissions to my underwriters to get a 20 percent discount on the fire rates. That 20 percent discount is why I sold insurance to all those pizza and sub shops because they all needed vent-system cleaning contracts. I created a company that did nothing but clean systems for the fire-protection systems inside vents for sub shops. I gave the job to that friend, of mine, and he did all the work and got all the money. I didn't get any money, of course, as that would have been a direct conflict of interest.

Remarkably, I made $68,000 in my first year because even though my income was only $9,000, I made great money in commissions. The company decided to groom me for management, so they sent me to SUNY-Binghamton to complete my MBA so that I could become a manager. That move changed the trajectory of my life most unexpectedly.

When I was at my MBA program, I met a guy who was a nephew of a politician in Venezuela. Once we became friends, we started going to the café and drinking beer all night instead of going to class. He happened to mention that his relative would probably like to buy stuff from us if we could set up an export company. Thus, the company I still run today, US-ABROAD, was started by two young guys drinking beer in a bar while they were supposed to be working on their MBAs.

If you look closely enough, you can see the invisible hand that directs you through your life, and you may not even know that's there. In my case, so many different possible things could've gone wrong along the way, yet somehow I was able to make ends meet and learn from the crazy circumstances I would be thrust into later in life, and not necessarily by choice. I don't regret the fact that I made mistakes, as I learned from them.

If you can forgive yourself, you can move on. When Caleb approached me that day in the park, the whole idea of forgiveness was new to me. All I knew at the time was that you get out what you put in, and you must work damn hard to get it out. I'd no idea the concept of grace existed; that you could get something that you didn't have to earn through sweat equity. Nor did I understand the concept of making a mistake and not having to suffer for it. I didn't feel forgiven, but I believed that I could be forgiven.

Forgiving yourself when you make a mistake is a necessary skill to develop if you're ever going to be able to forgive somebody else; you can't forgive other people until you can first forgive yourself. When you ask for help, you'll get it. So I asked for help when I was 18, and even though it didn't happen exactly the way I thought it would, I graduated from high school and college. Knowing I was forgiven and being able to push the restart button changed my direction in life. I recognized that I was the predator as the encyclopedia salesman and nobody was hurting me; I was hurting other people. When I was forgiven, I got a new start, and I never went back down that road again.

Doors opened for me. The grace that those church ladies had for me by reaching out and helping me start a business to clean carpets and support my family was undeniably life-changing. Anybody can have an opportunity, yet I made the most of the chance that I was given. The universe has conspired to help me ever since I made the decision that day in that New York park to be forgiven. I have no idea how it happened, and I don't understand it, but I'm sure that the invisible hand helped me, just as it helps you.

Fear will always whisper in your ear, "Let's play it safe. Let's get a good job. Let's save for our retirement. Let's compete for that job, even if we have to lie or cheat or steal." That's the kind of toxicity that people live their lives by in thinking that there's scarcity. In reality, the universe is standing by saying, "Everything will be fun, and you can make plenty of money. There's no scarcity. Everything's fine." Choose not to listen to the voice of fear; choose the voice of the universe instead.

When I look back at how I was as a young person, I still have that person in me. I still have that predator in me; I still have that fear in me. I still have that need to be unique; that need to be an individual. It's always there. I hear it, but I no longer listen. The concept of forgiveness and atonement means that the universe loves you and nothing is going to change that. Forgive yourself for listening to your ego, and choose to listen to the other voice instead. You can start over again as the universe knows your heart, and will help you if you decide to listen to your inner voice.

We create our pain and suffering because we can't forgive ourselves for our mistakes. My life was such a mess, and somehow the universe helped me in such a beautiful way. I want to show you that the universe does love you and takes care of you and all you have to do is say "Yes". Don't be afraid to follow that inner voice that's part of the universe. Learn to trust your intuition and wisdom.

CHAPTER TWO

GIVE PEOPLE ONLY AS MUCH INFORMATION AS THEY CAN HANDLE.

Give people only as much information as they can handle. We give simple instructions and recommend internal and external resources, but we do not overwhelm people with far more than they can process. Providing too much information leaves people feeling incompetent and unworthy.

When I was young, my parents were conscientious not to give me too much information. They felt that overloading me with facts and concepts and realities might stunt my ability to trust my intuition and judgment. Parents generally have a substantial effect on their children; a significant impact on how they direct them. Parents should be careful not to be too overpowering with their children.

When I was 9 or 10, I said to my mom, "I don't know what I'm going to be when I grow up."

She said, "I think you do."

"I don't have any idea," I said. "Do you have an idea?"

"I do."

I asked, "Well, what is it?"

She said, "You'll find out."

My parents knew exactly when not to talk, and when not to tell me what to do. As a kid, I felt that they knew everything but didn't want to give away the answer. Otherwise, I wouldn't learn how to find my answers. Perhaps my mother didn't know what I should do, so she just said she did and left me to figure it out on my own. She went along with the idea that I would know when it was time.

I think that might have been the same thing with my dad. He didn't have any idea what I should do. He was, however, smart enough to know he didn't know, so instead, when I asked him the same question I asked my mom, he said, "You'll understand when it's time." If we don't have preconceptions, and we don't feel like we need to know all the answers, it's not a bad idea to say, "I don't know."

That's also a good thing to do with your team members. If a person is facing a difficult situation and they think they don't have the answer — as long as it's not a specific technical issue that they need help with— in most cases they could figure out a solution on their own if they tried. Chances are if they don't know what to do, you probably don't know either. You have to have an open heart and an open mind. If you're sure of that answer, you shouldn't tell them unless there is no possible way they can figure it out.

At our company, we don't fire people. Instead, we encourage them to make mistakes but we create safety for them to be able to do so. Helping people to be happy when they make mistakes, giving them the freedom to think for themselves with a limited amount of direction, permitting them to establish reasonable goals, and then letting them fail to reach their goal in a small way is the cost of business development.

Our company provides morale Internet services for the military; we help people deployed in dangerous situations talk to their spouses, kids, family members and friends while we protect their privacy. Few companies go where we operate so we don't have many competitors — perhaps five entities compete with us as it isn't the type of business people are falling all over themselves to get into. I love it, but not everybody is gung ho to work in a war zone. Our end goal is, however, a crucial objective — to provide private connections so the military can communicate with their loved ones.

To manage people effectively, you must be able to get your ego out of the way so people are allowed to grow and develop on their own, find their voice, and discover their real gifts. If you can help a person do that, they're going to be worth a kazillion times more to you than they would if you have to scare them into working. People don't function as optimally when they operate from a place of fear. Acting from fear will always result in fear of taking a chance. The people who work from a place of love are going to be creative and productive and hopeful and fruitful.

There are two different ways to look at withholding information. One way is more effective than the other. For example, when my parents withheld their opinions as to what they thought I should do with my life, that was an excellent example of letting me figure it out for myself. Their actions helped me — that's the right way. There is also, however, a wrong way to withhold information and the following story about my selling CB radio antennas is an ideal illustration of how I helped myself by withholding information.

I'll then include two stories that illustrate the right way not to give too much information. The primary point about not providing too much information is that if you give too much information to people, they feel like you're going to expect them to do everything in the exact way you want it done. It's essential to build a diverse and creative corporate culture instead of a safe place. It's not that the safe homogeneous place to work is a bad thing, as it's not. It's not, however, the same thing as having a diverse place to work. The distinction is important.

USABROAD started as an export management company. As I mentioned, while working on my MBA, I met my pal, the family member of a Venezuelan politician. His relative was interested in buying school supplies from America and that required that I get an office, a telex machine and a secretary. At 24, I was the only guy in Binghamton, New York with a telex machine, as Binghamton just happened to be the territory I got with the insurance company.

Before the Internet, and before fax machines, there was the telex machine, which was a public switched network of tele-printers similar to a telephone network to send text-based messages. So, I had all those customers buying business insurance from me. I'd started an international business entirely by accident.

I started selling stuff to people around town for a company called Endicott Coil, which was a research company. The owner was probably the most creative guy I ever met, and because I had a telex machine, he would ask me to do various things for him and the next thing you know, I was in the export business. About six months into my new venture, I got a call from the United Kingdom from a guy in Manchester who asked, "Can you get me some disguised antennas?"

I didn't even know what disguised antennas were, but I said, "Sure, I can get you disguised antennas. How many do you want?"

"I need 3,000 of them. However, I can deal with 500 a week."

"What do you normally pay for them?"

He said, "I normally pay about $22 a piece."

"Landed or before freight?"

"Before freight."

I said, "We can do them for $11."

I just took the price and divided it by two. Although I still didn't know what disguised antennas were, I asked which model he wanted, and when he told me the model, I said I would put together the pro-forma quote for him.

I called some guys in New York who were in the business of closed-out merchandise and learned that the antenna the guy requested was a CB radio antenna. The CB radio boom had just ended six months before, and when I called, those antennas were closing out for 50 cents a piece. I sold three thousand antennas that I'd bought for 50 cents for $11, and that was the end of my insurance days.

Every week, I made five or six thousand bucks, which was a lot of money back then. At first, it was just my secretary and me, so I hired some guys from high school to help me as the business grew. We bought CBs for $10 a piece on closeout, took them apart, and shipped them overseas. They were not yet legal in the U.K. — which was one of the reasons why they were so expensive — as they hadn't passed the CB radio frequencies yet. The CB frequencies had to be licensed by the Post Office in the United Kingdom, and what was holding up the licensing of the CB frequencies was the Post Office's grip on bureaucracy.

I shipped the parts to one location, and the boards to another site and the rest of the components to still another place. Then I booked a flight on an airline called Laker Airways, which was one of the first discount airlines to fly between London Gatwick Airport and JFK for $98. On my first trip to Gatwick, I rented a Ford Fiesta, and even though I'd never been to the U.K., and I'd never driven on the other side of the road before, I made my way around and picked up all my radio parts. I was alone on that trip, and since I knew what I was doing, I went to my hotel room and put the CB radios back together again.

The next day, I found a truck stop, and I asked the first guy I saw, "Would you be interested in buying any CB radios from the United States? I just brought in about a hundred of them."

He said, "I'll take them all."

"How much do you want to pay for them?"

"I'll give you £80," he said.

"I'm not selling for £80." I didn't even know what £80 was, but I said, "But I'll sell them for 120."

He said, "Let's settle on 100."

So I agreed. Remember that I bought the CBs for $10. I sold them for £100 each in a lot of 100. That was $2.50 to the dollar, so I'd sold each one for $250, and I bought them for $10. At the top of the game, I had 20 guys doing the same thing, and we worked until the CB market blew out. By then, I'd a few million dollars to my name, so I bought a drilling company and went to Africa to start drilling water wells. I learned as a young man that it was so easy to make money as all you had to do was try anything and you would succeed. Life, however, had other lessons to teach me.

I want to share a story about a situation that happened much later in my career. It's a reasonably good example of how letting people think for themselves without giving them too much information created a better outcome than going down the road that I was on. There's a company that is now a financial and technical partner of ours in the Middle East, and is currently branching off with us into other markets in

Afghanistan, Bahrain and Turkey. They're lucrative, and with 120,000 employees, they've a lockstep way of choosing financial partners and getting people to work within their organization.

Their due diligence is multi-layered — technical, economic, security and disaster recovery. To get onboard with the company, you receive 400 to 500 pages of questions that you have to answer; you also have to provide documentation to support your answers. Onboarding is the term they use for having passed muster in every single layer of their company so that they can invest in one of your projects.

Well, we could never pass muster with them. The only reason that we got to be partners with them is that at some layer in their organization, they were more focused on meeting customer requirements than on achieving their internal due diligence. I tried for three years to get on board, and every single time, there was a layer called an ISO certification that I couldn't get done. That certification required us to have a disaster-recovery operation so that if our network went down, it would automatically be backed up and performed in some other physical location somewhere in the world that would take over.

Well, our network doesn't work that way. It's a remote structure of different kinds of cloud architectures that back up data on a moment-to-moment basis. All of our processes are backed up in six or seven different locations around the world every few minutes. This disaster-recovery mechanism is built right into our systems. We don't have a place that can fail because we have six different locations that work simultaneously to support each other. If one fails, we have five others to take over. If two fail, we've got four others to take over, so there isn't any one physical location that can go down.

Every single time we got to the disaster-recovery program document, no matter what we did, no matter how we explained it, and no matter how many times I wrote books about our system, we couldn't pass muster. We kept getting turned down on our onboarding process. I kept going back, however, and doing the same thing over and over again.

Then I hired people to do the same thing over and over again; to add additional explanations, new drawings, further engineering backup plans and so forth. I kept getting turned down because the same people looked at the same stuff and said, "This is not a disaster-recovery plan; this is global architecture, and it doesn't have anything to do with disaster recovery. So we're not going to approve it."

After three years, I hired Paul, a corporate type. He went through all of the same steps I went through while going through the onboarding process. He got to the same point, and he had precisely the same thing happen. We then hired a consulting firm for $10,000 to write a disaster- recovery plan that would meet the specifications. Unfortunately, it was turned down because it only explained what we did in different words.

Paul asked, "Could you let me handle this?" I gave the go-ahead, and would you believe that after several years of failing, Paul got us on board. He went to management and enabled us to escape from following their rigid corporate structure of filling out papers according to the way they wanted them filled out. Paul explained that our network didn't fit their onboarding process as their process was designed for an organization that doesn't do what we do. Our organization is not set up in the same way that the company has theirs set up, and he had to think of some way to get around the block.

Paul came up with the idea of skipping the onboarding document entirely. Instead, we would do a nondisclosure agreement, which would set us up as a technical partner that wasn't going to share information with anybody about what we were doing, and they weren't going to share any information about what we were doing either. At the end of the document, he inserted one little sentence that read, "This will constitute an onboarding approval on the part of the company." The document went up to their legal command, and everybody signed off on it, and that's how we got on board. We never had to worry about it again.

I'd never have come up with that idea. Paul's solution, however, was based on his years of corporate experience. He had a completely different background from me, and he wasn't trying to fit us into the corporate box. He used the organizational hierarchy and the organizational structure to get around the corporate structure: I didn't know how to do so. The next thing I knew was that we had a $10 million line of credit for funding new projects because of that crazy nondisclosure agreement he created.

In principle, we had to do something entirely out of the box by jumping the tracks and ultimately derailing the system to short circuit itself. If I'd given Paul a ream of information about how to solve the problem, it wouldn't have been resolved. I knew we were at an impasse, and I couldn't get us through, but Paul could, and it worked. This is an excellent example of the success of not giving people too much information because when I provide my knowledge, people think that they're supposed to do what I tell them, and we get stuck because people follow only my advice. If I didn't give too much information, we might have made it through this a long time ago.

Some of the countries where I do business have different social norms from those of the United States. Since social norms influence decisions more than a desire for fairness, this can cause problems in my business dealings. I often experience problems, but that's okay because I don't mind problems. The uncertainty that comes from my way of looking at things doesn't bother me. It doesn't matter what continent, country, village or family you come from. I don't see people broken down by nationality.

Another example of a time when I didn't give too much information was when the United States pulled out of Iraq, and the government was taken over by the Iraqis. The provisional coalition authority and all the mechanisms Americans put in place to structure the ongoing operations of Iraq were removed and replaced with an old-style bureaucracy that was based on Ba'athism. Concerned with renaissance, this Arab nationalist ideology is a form of socialism that promotes the development and creation of a unified Arab state. When Saddam Hussein was in power, the Ba'athist system was high-level and bureaucratic and highly regulated and controlled by an oligarchy of leaders.

Unfortunately, even though that was not the intention of the Iraqis, the country fell back into the same old pattern. What they've got right now is a complete mess of regulations that make absolutely no sense. They're top-heavy, tightly controlled and bureaucratic, and they tax the private sector to such an extent that it paralyzes their ability to grow economically as a modern power.

A megabit in America sells for about 78 cents. In the developed world, bandwidth for the Internet could sell for as little as 60 or 70 cents. In the Middle East, it's around $40. In Iraq, the price was $150 a meg because the Iraqi government placed $120 tax per meg on their bandwidth. Anybody that's sending Internet traffic through public routers has to pay the government $120 for every megabit that they sell. The average service right now in America from Verizon is a gigabit service, which is 1,000 megs. If we had to pay $120 a meg in tax, you'd be paying $3,500 for your home Internet service every month.

In Iraq, they have home Internet, but it's crappy. When you have to put $120 a meg on each megabit, then people use a fraction of meg in their house. It's like dial-up speed, but that's all they can afford because of the government tax. With a massive tax combined with dial-up speed, you can't get online. You can't do online courses; you can't do online banking. You can't do video services. All the things that we do in America that we take for granted can't be done in a market where they tax their bandwidth at $120 a meg.

CHRIS CATRANIS | 45

That's just an example of what happens when you have a so-cialist government that thinks, "Oh, this would be a good idea to make money for the government. We can use this for all these social programs," and then throw a $120 tax on some-thing that is going to cripple everything else in the economy. Aside from that, they've got a massive bureaucracy with ka-zillions of rules.

One of the things that I have to do to get operational in Iraq is to get my company registered with the Ministry of Trade, which in the U.S. is a 30-minute job that costs $300. You go online, fill out some forms, hire a registered agent for $150, and another $150 for state filing fees. Two days later, you get an employee I.D. number, and you've got a corporation, a cor-porate book, and everything that you need to start functioning.

In Iraq, I wanted to do the same thing as I have more than ten years of experience operating a company in Iraq. That lapsed after the U.S. government pulled out. I'm currently trying to get my company going again. Yet the amount of paperwork that I've been doing for this project is enormous.

First, I had to get an office, which cost $2,500 a month. After I hired an office, I had to hire a lawyer, which cost $6,000. After I hired the lawyer, I had to prepare five different sets of documents and have them all notarized by the Department of State in the United States, the Arab Chamber of Commerce and the Iraqi embassy in Washington at a cost of $3,000 per document — another $15,000. After I did that, I had to translate everything into Arabic and that cost another $5,000. All those fees plus the $1,500 from my manager for the first year added up to $85,000.

I submitted it all to the Iraqi government, and they said that I did it wrong and would have to do it all again. The five different sets of documents are supposed to be in five different authentication packages, and I had authenticated them all in one package. I was told to take them all apart, and get them reauthenticated as five different sets of documents. In that first year, therefore, I sent $85,000 down the poop shoot. Then the second year came along, and I'd separated all the documents and updated everything.

I handed the papers to my Iraqi employees, and they asked, "What should we do now?"

I said, "You figure it out yourself. Find a lawyer. Figure out how to get this through the system. I'm not going to tell you how to do it because I told you how to do it last year, and I spent $85,000, and I might as well have flushed it down the toilet. If you can't figure this out, maybe I shouldn't be doing business in Iraq. However, I think you can do it."

Those are my guys — a good friend and my general manager — who must figure this out. I'm not telling them how to do it. I'm withholding all the information that I think has to be done because I don't want to send them down another dead end that could cost me another $85,000. I don't know how it's going to work out, but it's a direct application of what we did with the other company for the onboarding process. I'm leaving the guys who are on the ground — those who know what's happening in Iraq a lot better than I do — to figure out how to bird-dog this through the government. If you don't tell people what to do and allow them to figure it out, they'll get it done.

CHAPTER THREE

DON'T TAKE THEIR POWER AWAY.

Don't take their power away. When we take decision-making power out of people's hands, we leave them feeling useless and incompetent. There may be some times when we need to step in and make hard decisions for other people, but in most cases, our staff members need the autonomy to make their own choices. We empower all staff to make their own decisions on behalf of the company. We offer support but never try to direct or control them.

I learned early in my career to accept the good ideas from my team members and extend power to others; it didn't just happen by accident. When I started USABROAD, I paid close attention to the weekly Trade Opportunity Program bulletin from the Department of State, as it identified who was importing what from where in the world. My people then wrote letters to the importers in our attempts to win business with us.

Our letter began, "Greetings from the staff of USABROAD. We're an international trading company specializing in the supply and delivery of X". Whatever was in the trade opportunity bulletin, we'd type in that product. It could be dogfish flaps and backs or shunt capacitor banks for nuclear power plants or sardines. Whatever it was, we were the experts in that letter. The letter continued, "We're not like the other guys. We want to help. We want to give you a CIF (cost, insurance and freight) quotation right to your country and take care of everything. We want to make sure that everything gets to you on time the way you want it. If you don't like it, you don't even have to pay." Pretty soon, we started to get business because nobody else used our approach.

I'd one guy who specialized in medical products, and when I looked, I saw that nothing was happening in his department. I looked at his letter and saw that he'd changed it to read, "There is a myriad of interfacing links in the realistic." I thought to myself that it was the most ridiculous thing I'd ever read in my life. We were never going to get an order if that was an example of the kind of letters we were sending out! Who would read that garbage? As I thought about that over the years, I thought it was a beautiful way to express what we were about. When, however, I looked at it in my late twenties, I fired the guy on the spot because he wouldn't change his letter. He was a few years younger than me, but he was easily 30 years ahead of me in thought.

I no longer remember his name, but I've always remembered what he did. He's probably the head of a company like Google by now. The point is that I had a goldmine with him and I didn't even know it, which is why you don't want to take power away from people; people who think out of the box in ways that are unusual and that are worth their weight in gold.

The onus falls on you to understand them, not the other way around. That freedom of thought stems from a place of love and support and positive things in their lives. That was not my life at that time, so I didn't understand what he meant.

At the beginning of my business endeavors, I didn't think of myself as a leader, let alone a disruptive leader. Now I consider myself to be a disruptive technologist who learned how to leverage government funding through EXIM bank funding. I leverage the funding to create a social impact wherever I go. The social impact starts with the people who are working with me and joining the mission wherever we are — China, Iraq, Kyrgyzstan or Nigeria. Everybody's a leader in my world; in my disruptive reality.

Since we do not fire people, if somebody doesn't work out in the company, instead of letting them go, we move them home and keep them on. I've had people on my staff for years now that haven't done what they were initially hired to do. We shift their responsibilities to something they can do, and since we can afford to do it, who cares? We're not going to fire people because they fail.

I know it doesn't make economic sense on the surface. It makes excellent financial sense, however, because when you say "Yes" to helping people and "Yes" to life, people and life help you back. Who knows how many ways we've improved ourselves by helping other people? Ever since we implemented this unorthodox policy, we've made more money than ever and making extra money means we can change the world in more ways as we can do more with it.

You don't make money by being cheap with people or firing people. You make money by being creative and encouraging people to be their best. You don't want people operating from a place of fear to get them to perform. The biggest concern our people have around employment is that they fail and get sent home and collect training pay with early retirement.

There are only two emoting drivers that cause people to do anything. One is fear, the other is love. If it's love, it makes positive change. If it's fear, it brings about toxicity and negativity. If you want to motivate people by fear, you're going to end up with a toxic working environment. People will be extending that atmosphere into everything they do and in all their relationships in every other part of their lives. If you're going to operate out of love, the worst that's going to happen to you is you're going to get taken advantage of from time to time.

I attended a seminary, so occasionally I rely on my seminary training to explain things. One of the stories that remains with me is the story of the rich fool in the Gospel of Luke. He becomes incredibly rich, and everything he touches turns to gold. He says, "What am I going to do? My barns aren't even big enough to hold all my wealth. I guess I'll tear down my barns and store all my wealth and then I'll be able to live fat and happy for the rest of my life." Then God says to him, "You fool. Your soul is going to be required of you on this night."

The rich fool amassed wealth and then died without any preparation. That's a simple story, because what happens when things start to work? Do we begin to think of how we can deploy those things into areas of social impact? Alternatively, do we sit around fat and happy? That's what makes it all worthwhile. If you're not focusing your wealth and your resources on social impact, where is your focus? If it's not focused on something to help humanity, you're only focused on self-gratification and investor profit and dividends, and it's toxic. That's where my interest in hydrogen-powered houses began.

We're learning to build houses run on hydrogen, but they're costly right now as they're early-adopter technology. We want to make sure that those houses will benefit the world as we help to transition home living from fossil fuels and the grid. Our goal is to control how much energy is consumed and monitor how we're producing energy in the form of hydrogen. We'll build a power company to connect all the houses.

You might wonder how I present the concept of hydrogen-powered houses to investors who are looking strictly for financial gain. Well, investors don't invest in my company because of dividends. They don't invest in my company to maximize their profit, as it's a high-risk investment. They know up front that if we do make money, we'll make a lot of it. Those who take a shot on our investment do it because they want to be part of the humanitarian mission.

For example, when we were operating in Iraq, most of our investors were lawyers and doctors from Long Island. They wanted to talk about what they were doing to try and help the effort when they were enjoying themselves on the golf course or in the country clubs. They threw in $25,000 here and $25,000 there. Those guys wanted to be part of the mission and didn't care about the money. We're not a nonprofit; we're set up for profit. We tell potential investors, "If we make money, it's going to be 20 times what you put in. If you can't accept a level of risk, you're not in the right place."

We function differently, our objectives are entirely different, and our message is different from most projects. We take on hard jobs, truly impossible situations, but we have fun doing it. We encourage everybody to be creative. We accept that we're not always going to win, and sometimes we're going to lose more than we gain. If you want to be part of that, that's great. If you don't want to be part of it, that's okay. There are plenty of people who want a piece. We're not, however, the kind of company where people are going to sit around in an investment club to try to figure out how to maximize their retirement fund.

I allow our people to complete the work however they want, wherever they want, as long as they get it finished. We don't have any office hours. All of our people work remotely unless they work at a military installation and they have to work on a base for their protection. In that case, we have office hours, but they're 24/7, and everybody has to rotate.

Most people have to work 12 hours a day, just like soldiers. When you deploy with troops who are on active duty, you've got to join them and participate and live in the same environment where they live. We use the same dining facilities and the same latrines they use. We have to understand the way they live and do the same.

Otherwise, everybody works remotely from home. It doesn't matter if they're doing call-center work in the Philippines out of their homes or in America. Everything's connected through technology. We don't have a water cooler where you can stand around and gossip, and you don't have to drive two hours in and two hours home. We'd rather have people spend time with their families. If you're going to be home, why screw with commuting or office politics? That's unnecessary and a waste of time.

We'd rather have people spending time getting certifications and studying to improve themselves in their line of work, especially around technical certifications, for which we have many people focused. They're not technicians per se, as a lot of them didn't graduate from high school. We're teaching them to become Cisco-certified network engineers, or network specialists in some area, whether it's VoIP, networking or Layer One stuff. Whatever we focus them on, we want them to get certified.

Sometimes they fail four, five or six times before they pass a test and we tell them that failure is the road to success. If they fail those certification tests, we're not giving bonus money, but we're certainly not penalizing them. We never punish people for failing. If they don't even take the test, they might lose their spot in that particular project and go home until we find another place for them. That, though, is the worst thing that's going to happen.

When people go home, they get training pay, which for an other country national (OCN) is $850 a month, the minimum payment we provide. As soon as they pass their first certification test, which is a CCNA, they immediately earn $2,000 a month. To put that in perspective, a typical OCN in the technology industry starts at about $300 to $400 a month. From the start, they're making more money with us as a trainee than they'd make even if they became a network engineer. A person in the Philippines who earns $850 a month could easily be making more money than practically anybody in their town. If they succeed, they make $2,000 a month, and it goes up from there.

By the way, we get lower prices for every CCNA we have on our payroll from Cisco-Meraki and our other vendors. The more certified people we have, the bigger our discount gets. We're trying to create a system that's like a self-licking ice-cream cone by which everybody benefits. Does this backfire? Occasionally.

Because we don't have the traditional idea of managers, we've got people who are in charge of other people. Although we call them supervisors, we don't call the people they supervise employees. We do, however, have people who have more authority to help others develop their gifts. Some of those guys have been through hell and back with me many times. If they hadn't become certified, and we'd lost our contracts, those guys would've gone back to driving vans or delivery trucks in Saudi Arabia for $300 a month. By working with us and getting certified, they can be hired by any company for $2,000-$3,000 a month. We know that even if we fail, our people won't fail; they'll still be able to take care of their families. That's the critical thing for us, not necessarily whether or not we keep our contracts.

If the fear of losing your contract does not motivate you, you generally do a better job than everybody else, and they renew your contracts. That's been our experience. If you're not worried about the deal and instead make your concern one of how to serve people, the better you help your people and don't worry about whether or not they like you, and they end up liking you more. Your customers like you more too, and you become more profitable and more successful.

If you keep that direction going, you don't have to worry about losing your contracts. If you miss one, you'll get three more. Is that counterintuitive? It's entirely logical to us. We feel we need to keep each other on track, so we don't take the freedom away from our people. If they want to leave, they can go as 100 others would take their spot if they leave. It's not like in the U.S. where you have 100 percent employment. The people that we draw from are from underdeveloped countries in Africa and Asia.

Our philosophy is so radically different from most companies. We encourage autonomy in the workplace by not discouraging our people from being autonomous. Naturally, people are independent. When, however, they get stepped on and pushed around and insulted and bullied and controlled and manipulated, that becomes the way of life. They expect it to happen. Organizations make up rules to make that type of behavior seem acceptable.

We don't define the boundaries of the control and decision-making power of our people. I'm not a big believer in limits; I don't like them at all, and I wish everybody would stop using that word because I don't have any limitations in my own life and I don't want to change that. Allowing our people to choose how to be autonomous is because we want them to think for themselves. Real power comes in a person's existence and acceptance and awareness of who they are as a beautiful creature with an infinite capability and potential. We want people to feel and believe that and remember who they are.

Once they see the space around what they think, they understand how infinitesimally small our opinions are. They see how little our problems are and how incredibly great the potential and possibilities are in the world. They start to think like that and open up to all kinds of great things. You don't want to take away that potential to open up to those great ideas and great thoughts. You have no idea what could come from individuals who feel they have the power to think and to act.

CHAPTER FOUR

KEEP YOUR OWN EGO OUT OF IT.

Keep your own ego out of it. This is a big one. We all get
caught in that trap now and then — when we begin to
believe that someone else's success is dependent on our
intervention, or when we think that their failure reflects
poorly on us, or when we're convinced that whatever
emotions they choose to unload on us are about us instead
of them. We will remain alert to our own tendency to
become more concerned about our own success (Do the
members of staff like me? Do their results reflect on my
ability to manage?) than about the success of our teams
in meeting their key performance indicators. To provide
sufficient support to our staff, we need to keep our own
egos out of it and create the space where our people have
the opportunity to grow and learn.

Backtracking to 1982, my intentions when I started my
import-export company were to make and save enough
money to start a water-drilling company. I was thinking about
world hunger and some practical way to create international
development in a developing country. I focused on Africa
because I didn't know anything about developing countries,

but I knew a lot about Africa because I watched a lot of Tarzan movies when I was a kid. Believe it or not, that shaped my thinking as an 18-year-old, even though it sounds silly now.

I wanted to start a water-drilling business in Africa, and while my experience in Africa turned out to be a complete disaster, it ended up changing my life in many ways for the better. As I said, sometimes looking back on whether you've been a success or a failure in any area of your life comes from how you look at it. If there's anything in my own life that represents the examination of the ego and my failure and success in any given endeavor, it's my time in Africa.

The import-export company was extremely profitable. Buying and selling CBs, I made more than $2 million within the first year. I knew, though, that it wouldn't last forever. I had 20 guys working for me — taking the radios apart, shipping them into the country, and flying over and putting them back together to sell them. We all accumulated quite a bit of cash.

My partner was a guy I'd known since junior high school, Tom Fletcher, and I asked him to work with me after he graduated from a Jesuit college in Berkeley, California. Tom was a philosopher, writer and poet. He came to work with me at the import-export company, and we made a lot of money. No matter what we did, we couldn't lose. There was way too much money to be made.

I said to him one day, "I want to start a water-drilling company in Africa."

Tom said, "Chris, we can do whatever you want, as you've got the money to do just about anything. You want to buy real-estate houses and be safe and live off people renting property? We can do that. You want to buy a water-drilling company and go to Africa and drill water wells? We can do that too. Whatever you want to do, I'm in."

I was young and optimistic, so I said, "Let's buy a water-drilling rig and ship it to Africa."

So that is precisely what we did. The only place where they spoke English and had oil money to pay for water was Nigeria. I could have gone to North Africa, such as Libya, but I wanted to go to Sub-Saharan Africa where I thought the real Africans were.

My African aspirations did not begin with a stellar landing, as shortly after I landed in Nigeria, I was beaten up and robbed. Then I fell sick with malaria, and while I was down for about seven days, I thought about ways to make my water-drilling business work. I wanted to do something that was meaningful to others, and because it had been nearly effortless to make piles of cash selling CBs, I figured everything I touched would be equally as profitable. Everything had been so easy up to that point in my life: selling books, cleaning carpets, moving CBs to the U.K. I had no reason to doubt that I would be every bit as successful in Africa.

After I recovered from malaria and regained my senses, I went to the U.S. Embassy and received from them a list of people who were looking to team with Americans. I visited each company on the list and eventually decided to collaborate with a company called Bedkana Block Molding in Port

Harcourt. We agreed to start a water-drilling company together. Port Harcourt is in the eastern part of Igboland.

There are three main regions in Nigeria — the West, the East and the North. The North is the home of the Hausa and the Fulani. The West is dominated by the Yoruba. The Igbo people live in the East. There are also hundreds of additional languages and dialects of those languages as well. Before European colonization, the Igbo were not united as a single people but lived in autonomous local communities. By the mid-20th century, however, a sense of ethnic identity was strongly developed, and the Igbo-dominated Eastern region of Nigeria tried to secede from Nigeria in 1967.

Under the colonial rule of England, the Igbo were the clerks who checked numbers. All the oil happens to be in the eastern part of Nigeria, which is why the Igbo eventually decided to secede. All of the wealth in the country was coming from the Igbo lands, and they began to question why they should give their wealth to the Yoruba. Because the Yoruba controlled the country, they were taking all the oil money from the Igbo.

The Nigerian Civil War, also known as the Biafran War, was fought between the government of Nigeria and Biafra. The Igbo people wanted to free themselves from the Yoruba-dominated federal government. Control over the oil production on the Igbo lands played a vital strategic role in the war.

When I was looking to do business in Nigeria, the Igbo had been wholly excluded from all the water schemes that the federal government in Nigeria had for the development of the country. They weren't getting any water wells, and there was no way to get government grants or government financing because they were being discriminated against because of the Biafran War.

I decided to settle in that area in 1982. It had to have been the worst place in Nigeria as they were being discriminated against by their own people. There were 100 million Igbo, and they were not getting enough water, and that was why I chose that particular area. I thought the area presented an excellent opportunity for my water-drilling idea. They had oil money, as well as a real need for water. Many Igbo walked five miles a day to bring home a few jars of water for their family, and the water was usually contaminated. I knew I could do a great thing in starting a water development project there.

When I started investigating how my idea was going to work, I was associating with Nigerians who were already well-indoctrinated in the Western way of administration and accounting and keeping inventory. I also thought they were trying to be Christian, and interested in adopting Western ways, and that it would make for a great match. On the surface, my idea looked like a great one, although I'm certainly not the first nor the last person to misjudge what appears to be an interest in Westernization.

Returning to America after my initial investigation, I bought a water-drilling rig for about $150,000, hired an engineer, and sent him and half of my import-export company to Nigeria. I told them that I would run the business from afar while overseeing their productivity and that when I could take the time away from the import-export business, I would visit. In

Nigeria, my team proceeded to start the drilling company.

We got some projects right away and succeeded in finding water. We were, however, paid in Nigerian naira, and there was no way to convert naira into U.S. dollars. Initially, that problem was just a speck on the horizon as we could spend and reinvest the naira in Nigeria, but the inability to convert it to U.S. dollars would eventually become a huge thing. I needed to pay my men in money they could use, and I also needed to send funds back to my family. We also, however, needed to purchase pumps, casing, additional drilling materials and replacement parts for the rig.

We needed foreign currency for those items. That's something that every company operating in Africa has to face. If there's no International Monetary Fund accord in the area, you must use local African currencies which are propped up by regimes and given an artificial exchange rate. The rate is controlled by an oligarchy of people who can get hard dollars. Only people with political power can import anything, and then they become the wealthiest people in the country. Even if you need a spark plug, you must go to one of those guys. Since they were the only ones able to import, I couldn't import anything on my own.

Right as the water-well business began to grow legs, my CB business fell apart. They legalized CB radios in the U.K. It had been that very lucrative market that had funded my African adventure. In the U.K., the radios were legalized on the FM frequency, and that rendered all of my equipment valueless. I had just invested about half a million dollars into the drilling company, and suddenly, I didn't have any more cash coming in.

In fact, not only did I not have any money coming in, but I had hired all of my friends from high school to help me out. I paid them well, and I didn't oversee carefully enough what they were doing. As I mentioned, I was still young and naive then. The guys were not crossing their *t*s and dotting their *i*s, where they should have been on purchase orders. I was discounting the purchase orders with the import-export Bank, and additionally, I was getting the funds in advance.

When it came time to collect the goods, we couldn't get our customers to collect because there wasn't any value on the frequency the radios were on. So we ended up with import-export Bank claims totaling more than $3 million with nothing to back them up because we didn't have any signed purchase orders. The short story is that this turned into a colossal disaster, and I lost everything. I never thought of bailing on my friends because I was just as guilty as they were on paper. I didn't forget to get signed purchase orders, but my friends weren't guaranteeing the notes that I was discounting; I was. I didn't watch, I was sloppy, and I wasn't very smart.

I didn't hold them accountable, however. It's one thing to make a mistake, admit it and let it go. It's another thing not to address it, and that's what I did because I didn't realize we were making mistakes in the first place. Fortunately, the bank didn't press criminal charges against me. I had nothing to claim at that point except the water-drilling company, which was the only source of revenue we had. Since we were making Nigerian naira, I couldn't have paid the purchase order debts with the naira.

As the purchase-order fiasco went down, I decided to head to Nigeria and take my place overseeing the water-drilling operation. Along the way, I came through Switzerland and stopped at L'Abri, an evangelical Christian organization founded by Dr. Francis Schaeffer and his wife Edith. Dr. Schaeffer was a Reformed theologian and a philosopher who brought relevance to the Christian message. The reason I liked the Reformed message was that they had a Protestant work ethic by which your duty in the workplace was your duty to God. This combination brought together my workaday world, my spiritual beliefs and my desire to do something meaningful. I left Switzerland feeling inspired and ready to change the world.

All of my high-school friends that I'd hired were not in the same headspace I was. They were young and crazy, like most young men. We were all in our twenties at the time, and we had just run through millions of dollars over the previous couple of years in the CB radio business, so money was not a problem. Even though all these guys from high school messed up with the purchase orders, I included them on my Nigeria project. I didn't make a conscious mistake at that point, but they were my friends, and as I saw it, we were all in it together.

The first evening I walked into our rented villa in Port Harcourt, I found all the guys in the living room smoking pot and drinking whiskey. Additionally, a strange parade of nude Nigerian girls was marching around the room while playing the bongos and tossing a Frisbee back and forth. They marched like soldiers in a circle around the guys. This was what I walked into. It could've been a scene from a movie.

I left that crazy scene in the villa's living room and headed upstairs to my bedroom, where I was later woken up at 2 a.m. to find a beautiful African girl hovering over me. I didn't say anything, because I didn't know what was going on, but it appeared she was there to stop the mosquitoes from biting me so I wouldn't get malaria. I'm not sure that acting as a human mosquito net was her whole intention, but I rolled over and went back to sleep and let her keep the bugs off me.

The next day when I went downstairs, the guys were already drinking this homebrew called kai-kai, a palm gin distilled to be about 190 proof alcohol. It was served with roots which were soaked in a punch. This drink allegedly prevented people from getting malaria.

Since I believed I was in Nigeria to stay, I got busy working with my guys on the drilling company. I brought over a new driller with me because the first one had quit by then. I learned several days into my stay in Port Harcourt just how wrong I was about my entire vision for Igboland. I couldn't have imagined that there were such deep cultural beliefs that existed in that part of the world, but I believed I could make my vision work. The ego, combined with naivety and youth, can do that to you.

Remember that I thought I was dealing with people who were interested in the Western way of conducting business. I learned that in eastern Nigeria, there was a cult called the Brotherhood of the Cross and Star, based in Calabar, which was about 120 miles from Port Harcourt. Olumba Olumba Obu ran the cult, and among other things, he claimed to be 190 years old and the sole spiritual head of the universe. By choosing Bedkana as a business partner, I happened to pick one of his apostles, and so indirectly, we had hooked up with one of the biggest cults in West Africa.

Most of the slaves brought to America were from Nigeria, and most had been sold into slavery by the Yoruba. A slave triangle was created, and how it worked was that manufacturers in New England would make rum. Then they would transport the rum to Africa and trade the rum with Yoruba chiefs. The Yoruba chiefs became powerful in Nigeria, and then would go to the Igbo lands, capture the Igbo people, and then sell those people as slaves. They worked on sugar- cane plantations in the Caribbean. The sugar cane was brought back to New England to make more rum, starting the whole cycle again — turning the rum into slaves, and slaves into sugar cane, and sugar cane back into rum, and so on.

Due to this terrible and tumultuous history, the prejudice that had existed from the 17th and 18th centuries between the Yoruba and the Igbo was still going on, and they remained enemies. My water drilling company was right in the middle of this, and of course, I couldn't have possibly known about this situation beforehand. From the exchanges of culture that happened between the New Englanders and the Africans, as well as the clash between animistic religions and the missionaries, we landed smack dab in the middle of an incredibly exotic form of cultism.

In addition to those dynamics, it happened to be an election year in Nigeria when I arrived bright-eyed and bushy-tailed and ready to change the world. Shehu Shagari was up for re-election for the NPN on the Yoruba side. The Igbo side was the NPP, and Olumba Olumba Obu was organizing all the villages in the eastern region to vote for the NPP candidate in opposition to Shehu Shagari, who was the incumbent.

That's where the story starts to get a bit strange. I didn't know this, but part of getting all those little villages whipped into political submission was to gain black-magic control over the villagers. With this type of power, the leaders could direct the actions of the people under them, and somehow they were able to do so. The guys from the Brotherhood of the Cross and Star would go into the cities and visit clubs such as the Blue Pelican in Port Harcourt. Every type of crook in the world found their way to that bar. The guys from the Brotherhood of the Cross and Star would go to the Blue Pelican to pick up prostitutes and entice them to go with them to the bush. There they would kill them. As they believed they could gain power from the spirits, the men would eat specific body parts in a cannibalistic ceremony. They thought that it gave them the ability to get the villagers to do what they wanted them to do.

All the Yoruba girls who were at the villa the night I arrived were juju priestesses in opposition to Olumba Olumba Obu or the Igbo leader. When the Americans moved into town, the girls thought they had it made and planned to use us to get the people on the side of Shehu Shagari, the Yoruba incumbent. Naturally, not only did I not know any of this was going on, I couldn't have imagined such a scenario was even possible. I was just a young man from upstate New York. Although I remained in Nigeria for four more years after this was happening, it took me a while to put the whole crazy scene together.

The head of the juju priestesses said we could help the villagers by bringing in water for them. She asked if she could go out in the rig with me and visit the villages, so I brought her along with my men and me. Once in the communities, she would gather the elders together.

I don't know why she said I was a Chinese engineer, but she told them, "This Chinese engineer will bring you water if you deny Olumba Olumba Obu."

They would ask her, "What does the Chinese engineer get out of it?"

She said, "You're going to pay him 20 naira per household."

20 naira on the black market equaled about $6 per household. In a village of 20,000 people, that meant about 5,000 families, and 5,000 times $6 was enough to drill a water well. The priestess was able to get the elders to support the idea of getting water to their village, and as long as the town was large enough, it would generally work.

We'd have a big discussion about how we were helping the people to get rid of Olumba Olumba Obu. In every one of these villages that supported the Brotherhood of the Cross and Star, the villagers had written over the doorposts of their door in white chalk "O O O" for Olumba Olumba Obu. My job in the process was to lick my thumb and wipe off the chalk from the first doorpost while everyone shivered in fear because he or she thought they would die as soon as this happened. After I was done taking the white chalk off the doorpost, I stood before them as they cowered, raised my hands in the air and yelled, "I set you free in the name of Jesus Christ!" and that sealed the deal. All the villagers were then required to renounce Obu before we started drilling. They had to wipe the "O O O" off the doorposts of their houses. All of the village had to comply, or there would be no water.

Then they would give us money, and we would start drilling water wells. If we didn't get water by the time we got to 200 feet, we'd collect money again to dig deeper. After we found water, we'd put in a submersible pump with a cement block structure around it. We put in a generator to power it to fill 5,000-gallon galvanized tanks on cement footers surrounded by spigots. The whole project was beautiful, bringing water to every household. If a family couldn't afford the $6 fee, there would always be some wealthy chief with money to assist them, so no one was excluded from the bounty.

Being paid in naira rather than U.S. dollars became a big problem as I couldn't convert the naira into U.S. dollars, so I started an ebony lumbering operation on the Cameroonian border. We were in Port Harcourt, which was at least a two day's drive from the Cameroon border. I visited few weeks. I had a bunch of barefoot, naked men chopping down ebony trees for me.

Only the center of the ebony tree, which is about 8 inches in diameter, is the heartwood. The guys took down those beautiful big trees and then hacked out the sapwood from around the core to reach the heartwood. Then they cut the heartwood into billets about four feet long, split those into four pieces and then dipped the ends in wax to keep them from breaking or cracking.

I would pay five naira (about a dollar) a piece for the ebony. The guys would pile them up on the lawn in front of my house in Port Harcourt. They'd hide billets in ditches and on the sides of the roads and dig holes for them in the jungle and cover them up. They'd hide them like buried treasure and wait for me to get back there so that they could sell the billets to me for a dollar a piece. When I'd fill a 20-foot container, which holds about 10 tons, I'd ship it to Germany as scrap wood.

My activity was written up in *Fine Woodworking* magazine, as I was the biggest ebony dealer in the U.S. at that time. I was working with a bunch of artists in upstate New York, one of whom was Rich Newman. They would take all the ebony that the Germans didn't buy and cut it up and sell it to people who made fretboards and piano keys. We had Gibson and Ovation and other different guitar manufacturers buying from us, and Rich loved doing it. It gave him a regular cash flow; he also made artistic furniture out of ebony, and one of his desks would sell for about $100,000 every few years.

So because I couldn't trade the naira, I financed my drilling operation by deforesting Nigeria; taking this rare, exotic wood for nothing and selling it for a hundred times what I paid for it. This process kept the operation going, but it was too slow-going to make a significant financial difference. I had 50 guys out there working for three months to fill a single container. Then there were issues around transportation and many risks on the roads.

When we started the ebony operation, it was because I had no political context. I was working on Igbo lands without any backing or political context. I had local indigenous workers, and I was drilling water wells with those guys in places where they weren't getting any government grants, and we weren't getting any government currency. Nothing around that situation was done the usual way, so we had to do everything out of the box. We collected money from the local people by going from house to house, and drilled wells based on receiving 20 naira from each of those families. There was no government involvement with any of this operation.

The currency issue was probably the most critical thing as we had to come up with a way to get our money converted into U.S. dollars. That was done through the ebony. Otherwise, we couldn't have functioned; we couldn't have bought pumps, bentonite or casing. We couldn't have paid anybody either.

It was in learning about the slave triangle that gave me the idea to create a functional operation. We would drill water, take the money from the water in naira, turn that currency into ebony, ship the ebony to Germany, turn the German cash into U.S. dollars, and then bring more parts and materials back to Nigeria to drill for more water. Then we would start all over again. I created the water triangle, which was like the slave triangle. It was just the opposite purpose, however, which was to bring water instead of making slaves. It did, however, involve deforestation.

The priestess was the brains behind this whole operation. She had us all under her control, and her girls were controlling everything we did. This was all fine and dandy except for one thing: remember, my chief was part of the Brotherhood of the Cross and Star and was one of the apostles who supported Olumba Olumba Obu. Our company was causing trouble as we were turning the villagers away from Obu so they could have water. Of course, I was paying my chief money every month, so it was a mixed bag for him to accept the funds but support our adversary. Eventually, it got to be a big enough problem that he decided he had to take action.

That winter there happened to be a yam festival taking place around Christmas time. The chief invited me and said there was going to be a wrestling match and he wanted to know if I would participate. The invitation wasn't entirely out of left field, as I'd recently wrestled one of the chief's sons in a compound where we happened to be working. I'd been a collegiate wrestler, and since I was in my twenties, drilling water wells and handling drillers and logging and carrying steel pipe all day, I was strong as hell, and in great shape, so I said, "Sure. Why not?"

Drillers' mud is called bentonite, and it comes in 50-kilo bags, and it takes hundreds of those bags to drill a well, as you have to move them around and pile them and empty them. That's great exercise, and of course, handling drilling casing also builds much strength. Sometimes we had to carry casing into a site because there wasn't enough room to get a drill rig in there along with the casing. That weighed hundreds of pounds, and it took three or four guys to carry each piece. I worked with the guys on the crew and did everything they did. We were continually flushing our well of water, so we carried lots of water around. We had a van that did nothing but pump water out of some waterhole and brought the water to the site. Then we filled water barrels and had to handle those.

In other words, drilling water wells is a lot of manual work. If you work on a water drill or water rig or any drilling rig, you're going to end up in excellent physical shape. As I mentioned, I'd been a collegiate wrestler and was captain of my wrestling team when I was in high school. So when I heard about this wrestling match in the village, I didn't have any fear until I found out who I was wrestling. I didn't realize that I was being set up. The guy opposing me was almost 7 ft. tall, yet I'd already accepted the challenge when I found out who I was wrestling. Not only did I worry this guy was going to kill me; I'm not kidding but his goal indeed was to kill me.

When I learned about this plan, I said to the priestess, "I have to get out of the country. I can't stay here and die."

She said, "No. You can't leave."

"What am I going to do then?"

"Don't worry," she said. "You'll be fine. I'll take care of it."

She stepped up my kai-kai for the morning. If you drink too much of that stuff, you hallucinate and do whatever you are told to do. So when it came time for the yam festival, the priestess took me to the village and gave me some special herbs to eat. I don't know what they were, but they made me ten times stronger than I was.

When I fought that 7 ft. guy, I won the contest and was crowned chief because I won the wrestling match in the village. The plan backfired on the Brotherhood of the Cross and Star as they tried to kill me, yet I became a chief instead.

As you can see, every time my ego led me into a more significant failure, I failed. I thought that I was going to be drilling successful water wells and save all those poor Africans from thirst. I lost my gold rush CB radio business. I ended up like Humphrey Bogart and the African Queen with this drilling rig in Nigeria. Let's not forget that my company was being taken over by a bunch of witches, yet somehow they helped us accomplish our goal to bring water to 20,000 people. It was the most significant and worst thing I ever did in my life.

It was, however, a mix of the genuinely bizarre that didn't seem like it was ever going to straighten itself out. During my next trip back to the States, my wife said, "If you're going back to Nigeria, your family's going with you. You're not going by yourself." We went back together for the next year, and then there was a military coup, and two more after that. Eventually, I had to eliminate all the juju priestesses from having anything to do with our company. By the way, the NPN won the election. Then there was a military coup, and the NPP overthrew the NPN. Everything went downhill from there. In 1987, after five years, I rounded up my guys. We were functioning at a subsistence level at that point, but the company was still making a living for everybody. I told them I wanted them to keep it going so I gave the company to my Nigerian manager, and I gave my boots to my driller, as well as the keys to the rig.

I left the country, and thought that everything was going to be fine, but the poor manager was killed by the chief who owned Bedkana about three months after I left. They murdered him, took over the company, fired all my guys, and took over the rig. So it didn't work out for anybody the way I had hoped, and I was very discouraged by the result. I lost all the money I made in the CB radio business when I was in Nigeria. I came home with $15 in my pocket, and I didn't know what to do with my life. My wife picked me up from the airport, and we went home to our house in Binghamton.

My time in Nigeria was so unsettling that I became wholly disillusioned about my mission to help the poor Africans. They'd tried to kill me, and worshiped devils, and ate each other, so it was a little bit hard to feel sorry for them after a while. I decided that the only way to bring about positive change in this world is to see people's hearts change from the inside out. I learned that it wasn't a matter of giving them water, nor was it a matter of giving them food or giving them jobs or making money. Some internal transformation needed to take place.

I said to Beth, "I think I want to go to seminary." I had decided that there was no way to bring about substantial change in people in those cultures without the Protestant work ethic. I wanted to go to a Reformed seminary so I could learn how to teach that to people. I believed that the best thing I could do would be to hang up my entrepreneurial guns and go to seminary and learn how to help people become followers of Jesus Christ.

My idea of following Jesus Christ was to work hard and build good businesses to support missionary work to help other people change. That was the Protestant work ethic that I bought into. It's not the message of Jesus at all, but I thought it was back then. The education was a long process. I worked for that degree for the next five years as I had to work part-time.

When I finally went to the committee that reviews licensure candidates for the presbytery, they asked me, "Mr Catranis, why are you interested in being a messenger of the Gospel of our Lord and Savior, Jesus Christ?"

I said, "Well, I'm not interested in that. I'm more interested in international development."

"Why, what do you mean?"

"I want a life like you," I said. "I want a career where I can be home every night for dinner and start at 70 grand a year and work one day a week. Then I have time to work on international development stuff."

"Chris, you're the second in your class. Is that what you think?" they asked, incredulous.

"Yes. I'm not going to lie to you."

They said, "You sound like you think this is a regular profession."

"It is."

"Well, Chris, you'd better go find a different profession because you're not going to work out here," they concluded.

So that was the end of my seminary days.

As you can see, I've experienced many failures in my life. Africa couldn't have been more of a disaster. How, though, can I encourage other people to fail if I'm not willing to fail too? How could I have learned to keep my ego out of business without such a colossal failure of my own? That's why we are a company of second, third, fourth, fifth chances, and failing around here is okay. We understand that you have to keep your ego out of it, and fail your way to success. That may sound counterintuitive, but it works.

Each of us has a part that thinks it's unique, and that's the ego talking. It assumes we're special, and thinks having individuality is the main thing that we have instead of having unity with each other and with our creator. The incredible focus on materialism and on the things that we can see and touch doesn't serve us. It's that focus point, however; the idea that distracts us from being able to get past our real ability to live and enjoy life the way we're supposed to.

When I use the word ego, I don't think of it as a good thing. I see ego in the sense that we have these two different pulls, one based on love and the other based on fear. I understand the ego as based on fear, and that's the one that I don't like. The pull based on love is an entirely different side of us. It's the aware, enlightened side of humanity with the inner voice that everybody has that completely contradicts everything that the ego says. Whatever the ego says is nonsense. Even if it sounds good, it's nonsense. Everything coming from that loving side of us is from the inner voice you want to heed.

Johannes Kepler said, "I was merely thinking God's thoughts after him." Then Albert Einstein said, "I want to know [God's] thoughts. The rest are details." The only things that matter are the things that never change. Moreover, the only things that never change are God's laws and God's principles. We cause our suffering by engaging in distractions that don't matter. The things that Albert Einstein called details become our focus, and we lose focus on the critical stuff when we focus on the details of life. You'll miss so much if you don't.

The things that do change, whether it's a human body or world governments, don't matter to me. The idea that matters is what doesn't change. When Albert Einstein said, "I want to know God's thoughts and the rest are details," that describes the same way I feel. God's thoughts are our inner voice, and our ego controls all the other details.

My ego says, "I want to change the world positively. I want to bring about positive social impact by using disruptive technology and leveraging it with the resources that I can find that are available to me and within my reach." That's where I want to put my focus; that's my ego. Essentially, that's an egoistic goal and aspiration of mine which doesn't matter. It's nothing. It's empty. It might sound good but it's my ego talking.

The real core of life is not to focus on that part, but to focus on the space around that thinking. Every lousy idea that ever came out of my mind came from my ego. Say you have writer's block, and you walk away from your table for a while and stop thinking. When you come back, something comes to mind out of nowhere that solves the block. That's the experience of going to this space; of going to the creative part of us; of going to the part where we know God's thoughts and the rest are details. You don't have to come up with an idea; it comes to you.

That's where I want to be, and moreover, that's where I want my people to be. The last thing I want to do is impose my leveraging disruptive technology with EXIM Bank financing to create social impact, and then force that down people's throats and say, "Look, this is what you've got to focus on." I don't want that. That's my ego. I don't have to bring other people into my reality. They've got their reality, and I'd rather learn about it.

Keeping your ego out of it means first of all recognizing that you have an ego. You must understand that you've got this negative thing going on inside. It may not appear negative all the time, but it can cause complete disarray and disruption to everything that's possible in your life because it's all based on opinions and perspectives that are ever-changing. They don't matter; they're just details.

Everyone is unique and unusual, and we can accept each other the way we are. We don't have to have all these differences of opinion because they're irrelevant. The only thing that matters is the love that we have for each other and our children and the things that are important in the world. Those are the things that last; that's our legacy, not our ideas and opinions. We have a split brain; one side is awareness, and the other side is the ego. If you listen to your ego, you're going to be walking down the road to fear. If you listen to your inner voice, you're going to follow the path to love.

I know that's typically not what you'd find as a thought in the business world. I've learned, however, that it doesn't work to focus on the outcome. That's a distraction from the reality of what the real purpose of the world is about, and that's to go through this classroom where there's pain and suffering, and learn to transcend it. You don't transcend it by trying to fix the classroom. You transcend it individually with what goes on inside you and the people you touch and who touch you. Then we transcend in unison, and we all work together, helping each other move forward. That doesn't happen by changing the outer world; it happens by changing our inner world, and by keeping our ego out of it.

CHAPTER FIVE

MAKE THEM FEEL SAFE ENOUGH TO FAIL.

Make our people feel safe enough to fail. When people
are learning, growing, or going through transition,
they are bound to make some mistakes along the way.
When we — as their mentors and leaders — withhold
judgment and shame, we offer them the opportunity to
reach inside themselves to find the courage to take risks
and the resilience to keep going even when they fail.
When we let them know that failure is simply a part of
the journey and not the end of the world, they'll spend
less time beating themselves up for it and more time
learning from their mistakes.

You probably know by now that I feel safe enough to fail. I
take my experience for what it's worth, learn value from
the mistake, and move on to my next endeavor. A crucial
element in running my company, however, was learning how
to convey that uncertainty to the people on my teams in a safe
and effective way.

In our company, success is rewarded, and if a person fails,
they're told about the mistake but not punished. Nothing sig-

nificant happens until you get comfortable with a high level of uncertainty. If you position yourself so that errors are standard and accepted, you've room for something entirely unexpected and completely wonderful to happen. It wouldn't happen if you didn't put yourself in a situation where you were lost, and you didn't know where you were going.

Unless you feel safe enough to take risks, nothing significant will happen. You must put yourself out there, and allow yourself to be vulnerable. Sometimes you're going to lose, and you might lose more often than you win, but the trick is not to mind the losing or the hurt. It's all part of the experience of living life.

Have you heard of the graveyard spin? Pilots and underwater divers can experience spatial disorientation by which they're unable to determine their actual position, motion and altitude. An illusion is created, and the person has the feeling of spinning in the opposite direction. The natural reaction is to counter the corrective measures, but that's the opposite of what they need to do. It's similar to driving on ice; the fewer corrective actions you take, the better.

When people find themselves in a graveyard spin, they let go of the helm, rather than continuously trying to correct the spin. They have to know precisely when to let go, but that comes from listening to an inner voice. You must know just how far to go, and that comes from listening to your inner voice. You have to have an open heart, and be willing to accept that what's in front of you is what life is teaching you at that particular point. Generally, my experience has been that the universe conspires to help you to get through whatever you're going through.

Every year, there's an innovation dinner hosted by one of our investors in Qatar, and I always attend along with a large group of executives from all over the world. We sit at round tables in groups of five or six people, and talk about how our organization innovates, and we share what our company does. After dinner, there's a paid speaker, such as Tony Robbins, who talks about innovation. Afterward, there's a trade show where we see all the new ideas for the year from all around the world.

At a recent innovation dinner, I was seated at a table with a group of generals and colonels, one or two other contractors and another executive from a telephone company. We went around the circle, and we took turns speaking about how our organizations were innovating. When my turn arrived, since our organization functions differently from most, I couldn't share much of a plan for how it all works, so instead I asked the group if they were familiar with the graveyard spin. I told the story about how we utilize the graveyard spin, and everybody laughed hysterically about that being the way we run our business; that we make mistakes that turn out to be successes by taking our hands from the wheel.

Another illustration of how we allow our people to feel safe enough to fail requires that I backtrack to the steps I took after the Africa failure and my experience at the seminary. After those failures, I decided to return to what I knew. I went to the Middle East, and started selling satellite dishes in Kuwait, which turned out to be a boom market. As with the CB radios, I made a lot of money and a good name for myself in the area. Since it was right after the first Gulf War, we called our company Patriot Satellite, naming it after the Patriot Missile so the Kuwaitis would associate our company with something positive. It was a great marketing strategy, and we soon became the biggest satellite retailer in the whole country.

It's important here to mention the Internet of things (IoT), a network of devices that can include vehicles and home appliances that contain electronics, software, sensors, actuators and connectivity which allows these things to connect, interact, and exchange data with each other. My interest in Internet connectivity began around this time and has influenced what has now become a great interest of mine — hydrogen houses. Standard devices, such as desktops, laptops, smartphones and tablets, can be embedded with technology to communicate with each other and interact over the Internet.

After I left Kuwait, I started a company called Skyway Partners. They used to build voice, video and data systems for apartment buildings. Starting with the experience we gained from Skyway, over the next ten years we went on to develop a new vision in which we combine the best of technologies in proxy servers, cloud management, firewalls and traffic management in a new technology called software-defined wide-area network (SD-WAN). This happens to be the technology that I'm currently working on with vendors from Switzerland. They're going to be rolling it out for us. We've already bought our first five appliances and started rolling out in Iraq, Lebanon and Qatar. This connectable technology can run over satellite or conventional terrestrial networks, or can be run over radio links. Currently, we're using a combination of radio links and fiber-optic cable and submarine cable under the oceans with the Swiss company.

We'll be building smart houses that will run on hydrogen, and connecting them over the SD- WAN-based satellite network to control all the energy they produce and consume. I imagine that eventually they'll be built all over the world, but they're costly right now as they're currently an early adopter technology. We want to make sure that when we create these houses, we can carefully control the energy consumption, as we will be able to manage and monitor how we're producing the energy which will run these homes. We will be building a virtual power company that connects all the houses so we can control the energy flow.

We plan to do this through the Internet, but not the public Internet so we can avoid hackers. Power companies right now are at massive risk concerning the national security of every country, because just about any high-school student can hack into the power grid and cause havoc. Those companies spend millions trying to figure out how to keep people safe from being hacked and having the energy grids come down. If an enemy wanted to take down the national power grid of the United States, they could do it. So what would America do if they didn't have power for ten days? The whole country would fall apart.

I don't want that possibility with my network, so you can't hack into the public network and get to us. We're creating our own Internet. This Internet isn't going to be terrestrially run by cables and fiber; it's going to be a satellite network.

We're going to rent transponders on satellites, and we're going to connect all the houses by satellite.

To return to the years right before the tech crash in 2000, we had more than 2,000 properties signed up when the market crashed. We had to have a certain amount of capital coming in all the time because we were building networks faster than people were ramping up because a lot of them were new construction. It would take six months to fill an apartment complex after it was built. In the meantime, we had the lease payment on all the equipment that we made, so we had to keep raising money to continue expanding. I was going back to the trough repeatedly to raise more capital.

When the tech market crashed, and Nortel went from $52 to $0.50 in 90 days, everybody panicked, including me. I couldn't believe what had happened. I was just as scared as everybody else. When my board saw how frightened I was, they fired my whole Skyway Partners management team, including me. Then they took all of our networks, and sold them for 10 cents on the dollar.

Back then, however, I couldn't let those investors know when we hit the bottom of the rollercoaster that we were going to come back up again. I didn't believe it myself, so how could I communicate it to them? I wasn't feeling safe enough to fail. The real-estate and investment guys knew the ups and downs of markets and wanted to follow the No. 1 rule of letting your profits ride and cutting your losses short. That's all they knew, and that's what they were following when they saw me not knowing what was going on. I didn't know as I didn't have the same philosophy I have today where making money and losing money are different ends of the same sausage. If you want to be in technology, you've got to be willing to do both; I didn't know that then, and I couldn't do it, so I lost. I lost my job, and I lost my company. I lost everything.

That company was underwritten by a famous hedge-fund underwriter that financed Dish Network, Microsoft and Skyway Partners. Dish and Microsoft made it through. They had leadership that knew that if they persevered and went through it one step at a time they were going to make it to the other side. I was too young and too inexperienced to know what to do.

Many people made it through, but I didn't as I got caught up in a graveyard spin, and I didn't know how to get through it when the tech market crashed. I was in excellent company, as only a few excellent managers were able to get their companies through the crash. I panicked, and it became one of my more significant failures. I lost $60 million. I'm glad I went through it and got a taste of it as it was an incredible experience to eat that end of the sausage.

Subscriber Networks (SUBNETS) was created between the tech crash of 2001 and the Iraq war of 2003. SUBNETS is still operating today as we never closed it, but allowed it to remain dormant until about three years ago when we revived it as a provider of managed network services. SUBNETS is alive and well today and is now the company that will provide all the SD-WAN services for my international community of hydrogen houses.

I stuck it out through the tough times. At first, I tried to manage those networks that we'd built before our team got fired by the board of directors. A lot of them weren't, however, willing to work with me. I'd already led them down the road to chaos once before, and they weren't willing to listen to me again. I only salvaged three of my old networks and the billing revenue on three networks wasn't enough to support my family and my son Luke's family and we were all struggling.

When the planes hit the World Trade Center, my fortune changed. I remember my dad said, "Wherever there's war, there's money." So as soon as the Iraq war started in 2003, I was on the next plane to Kuwait. I took a taxi to the Iraq border and walked across with nothing but a Thuraya phone and $7,500 in my pocket. I didn't speak any Arabic, so I took a taxi to Basra and hired a guide. I paid him $5 a day, and while we traveled around for 30 days, I decided I was going to bid against the biggest cell-phone companies in the world to win the mobile-phone license in Iraq.

I started a company called Babylon Telecommunications, Inc. (Babtel). When Skyway went down, we had many networks we'd built to provide voice, video and data on small and discrete networks. They would compete with the big telecoms and give landlords the ability to control their revenue for voice, video and data at their apartment complexes (that's similar to what we've been doing since 2004 at military bases.) This focused on enriching the landlord, who provided the financing by signing the lease for the equipment that we needed to build the network, and then we split the profit with the landlord.

I had no idea what I was doing, and was flat broke and entirely down and out. Somehow I had this idea that I could win Iraq's mobile-phone license. In Kuwait, I talked to a guy with whom I used to sell satellites. He was on board with my idea, and his family fronted me with a $200 million bond to post for the bid, and Babylon Telecommunications, Inc. was born. They invested $50,000 so that I could propose our services.

Of course, we lost, but that got me back on my feet in Iraq. I created Babtel for the mobile-phone license bid, and raised $200 million for that. It failed and turned into a pirate Wi-MAX network, which eventually morphed into doing BLECs on military bases. I spent the next eight years there working with the guy as he was awarded a $7 billion contract with the U.S. government, delivering food and water to the bases. They hired Babtel to do all of his VoIP phones, so I got into the data business bigger than ever.

The businesses we created in developing the first video and data networks was Subscriber Networks, which eventually morphed into Babylon Telecommunications. All the companies I created, including Skyway Partners, Subscriber Networks and Babtel (all part of USABROAD), were considered to be operational units of our overall BLEC networks. I was the first person to create a BLEC. The first BLEC company was Skyway Partners.

The security companies I worked with were a rough group of guys, yet together we built a market network in the middle of Baghdad that serviced and connected all the security companies so that they could use my phone service to any destination in the world, regardless of its particular cultural differences with other Middle Eastern states. When the U.S. military heard what I was doing, they hired me to work on the bases to protect the U.S. soldiers' conversations from being overheard by the local mujahideen or our enemies. They hired me to encrypt everything so nobody could eavesdrop on what the soldiers were talking about with their families.

I was given 16 different bases and all of a sudden I was back on Easy Street again. We were making so much money, and it was like nothing I had ever experienced before. I was, however, doing most of these networks on a concessionaire's basis, so I had to raise the money myself to build the network. Then I would share about 10 percent of my revenue with the U.S.O., even though they didn't put up any of the money for the networks. I raised all this money by telling the story to doctors and lawyers in America; I told of what we were doing through networking. I had a bunch of investors from Lebanon too. I raised millions of dollars from these two groups and built all those networks.

In 2011, President Obama pulled the troops out. As a result, I was out of pocket millions of dollars in all these networks, and broke again. Everybody lost their money because I was spending the money on networks as fast as we were making it. It was almost a blow-for-blow replay of what had happened to Skyway during the 2001 tech crash. I thought the war was going to go on for 20 years. We all did, as that's what George Bush said would happen. We lost everything when they pulled out. I packed up all my stuff, put it in storage off Balad Air Base s in the center of Iraq, and moved to Amsterdam with about $50,000 in my pocket to be with my family. I knew I had to start all over again.

I started looking for more bases that I could sell my services to and find money to raise again. I found a base in Kosovo called Camp Bondsteel that wanted an Internet service. After Iraq, when I was trying to raise money for the Kosovo project, I told my Lebanese investors about it, and they said, "Come on down. We'd love to take a look at the project." So I flew down to Lebanon, and when I came through the airport, I got thrown in prison. Some of my Lebanese investors weren't happy that they'd lost their money in Iraq, and they planned to hold me in prison until I paid back the $870,000 that they'd lost.

My son Lucas worked on trading all of my inventory — worth $5 million — to those guys for $870,000 so they would drop the charges. As terrible as this experience may sound, however, while I was in prison, my most life-changing event happened. They threw me in a 9 X 9 ft. cell with nine other guys. When we lay down, we had to snuggle up with each other to share blankets, even though it was the middle of June 2012, and it was hot as hell inside that cell.

The young men in prison with me were beaten every day, as most of them had been arrested for drugs. At the time, however, the U.N. was paying the Lebanese government $25 a day for every person they held, so as soon as they got a hold of somebody, they tortured them into giving them the names of their other friends. Then they could arrest them to keep the cycle going because they could only keep each guy for two years. The jails were overrun with young men who had not done much wrong.

The first few days in that Lebanese prison, I sat there completely confused about what had happened to me, because up until that point, life had been so lovely to me. All of a sudden, everything went wrong. My wife of 35 years left me after saying she couldn't take it anymore. My oldest son (a partner for 14 years) kicked me out of the company. I was in prison. Everything had come undone in my life, and I didn't have a dollar to my name. Around me, those poor guys were tortured and crying, and they didn't want to turn on the light because it was too hot.

There was no air conditioning; not even a window. There was only a toilet in the corner of the cell; just a porcelain hole in the floor. Maybe I was hallucinating, but when I was half asleep, I felt a voice in my heart say to me, "Chris, get up and clean the toilet." I don't know exactly how to explain this, but it was an inner voice, and I can't say what it was or what it wasn't. Despite my time in seminary, I'm not particularly accomplished at being religious, but I do believe that there's an inner voice in everyone. Moreover, if they listen to it, it will guide them.

I thought it was God speaking to me, so I said, "God, if that's you, I went to seminary for five years, so can you at least tell me something a little theological?" I didn't know what to think, and I tried to ignore it for a long time. The voice persisted, "Clean the toilet." It was like trying to ignore that *Hulk* magazine advertisement about buying the submarine but cleaning the toilet didn't sound like a fun thing.

Finally, I gave in. A church volunteer had come by that day and dropped off some towels and shampoo, so I ripped up the towels, and using the shampoo I scrubbed that toilet. That was no picnic as nobody had cleaned it for 20 years, and it was solid brown, covered in feces and urine. It took me hours, but when I finished, I felt very good about what I had done. Moreover, at last, the voice stopped.

The young men in the cell started to peek out from underneath their covers. Up until that point, we were in that dark room with no air conditioning, no light and no window, while everybody cried in pain under their blankets. That all stopped. Little by little, they peeked their heads out and then they sat up and everything changed in under an hour in that prison cell.

I was 58 years old, and they were mostly teenagers or 20-year-olds. I looked at one guy, and spoke to him in Arabic. Pointing to a vent near the top of the wall, I said, "Why don't you clean that off and see if it cools down in here?" He cleaned the vent, and the temperature dropped about six or seven degrees. That's noticeable when the temperature's more than 100 degrees.

It felt like the air conditioning had come on and then people started laughing. They were smiling. You know that song by Simon and Garfunkel — "The Boxer"? Well, I don't know what came over me, I just started singing that song, and when I got to the chorus, all the Arab guys began singing the chorus with me. Soon, the whole prison was singing in the middle of this horrible experience in which we found ourselves. All of our clothes had been taken because people try and hang themselves with their garments, so we sat in our boxer shorts in that prison cell and sang. When they heard the singing, the guards yelled, "Get that American guy out of here!"

I was immediately moved to one of the worst prisons in the world. Roumieh Prison is the largest and most notorious of Lebanon's prisons. Although it was initially designed to hold 1,050 inmates, today it's operating at 300 percent capacity, and it wasn't much different then. I was wondering what had just happened to me, but it didn't take me long to figure out that Roumieh Prison was where all the spies, terrorists and worst criminals are sent. I was put in a jail cell with the worst criminals in Lebanon. One guy had been arrested with five tons of heroin. Somebody else was in for murder. I guessed that you were rewarded in the jail for being there a long time, as the guys with seniority had the best cell, and somehow I ended up in their cell.

There were only five of us in there, and we had our bathroom and our kitchen as I was with the Rockefellers of the Lebanese prison system. My reputation preceded me as they were genuinely happy to have me there and they warmly welcomed me. Believe it or not, in that prison I made some of the best friends that I ever made in my life. One of the guys in the cell was in charge of the prison store, yet he was a criminal too. There was no way for people like me to get food and water because in Lebanon, they don't provide for prisoners; it's the family's responsibility. Since my family wasn't there, I didn't have anybody to provide for me.

My cellmates hooked me up with the guards, and the guards hooked me up with some mobile phones and a bunch of SIM cards which they gave me on credit to start to distribute around the floor to the other inmates. My son Peter wired some money to one of the families to cover some of the expenses, and that's how I got started in my underground mobile-phone business in Roumieh Prison.

The way it worked was that I got the guy at the prison store to accept cell-phone minutes for food and groceries. So if somebody was in jail and didn't have any money like me, they could get money wired in the form of minutes into their SIM card that they would carry with them. I didn't charge them for the SIM cards, and I didn't charge for the phones either, as I just put them on the floor and owned them all. Those guys would call home, and every time they used the phone, I'd get a share of the minutes. With the minutes that came in, I made about $75 a week at my peak and was living like a king. The income provided for everything, and I even had my own cook. On $75 a week, you'd be surprised at how you can live in a Lebanese prison.

I was having a great time making money again despite my circumstances. Eventually, my son got all the equipment sold off or traded, and once the Lebanese investors had been fully reimbursed, they dropped the charges against me. My oldest son — the one who kicked me out of the company — got me out of jail. When that happened, the guards came and arrested me for operating the cell-phone business. The same guys who were working me detained me and took all of my inventory. They transferred me to a military prison right before I got released for my bail, so I spent the last two days of my jail time in a Lebanese military prison stripped down to my birthday suit under lights and camera 24 hours a day. It was even worse than Roumieh.

I could never decipher precisely what happened, but I learned the lesson at that particular point in my life. If I look for that toilet to clean every day, it changes everything. Do that one thing that has to be done that nobody else will do. I go to the worst spots in the world and do the worst jobs that anybody could do, yet I have fun doing it. Every day I look for a toilet to clean and every day some toilet shows up that I have to deal with. I clean one every day, and every day something good happens.

In 2012, when I was flat on my back in a Lebanese prison, not a single member of my board of directors would even send me a bottle of water. When I got out of prison in October of that year, I followed the crumbs along the trail, and little by little, I brought the company back to life. In 2013, my son Luke resigned from Babtel, so USABROAD took it over. We built it back to where it is today, using SUBNETS to design all the network architecture and technical solutions.

Today, USABROAD is the main company and SUBNETS Is 40 percent owned by USABROAD, with 32 percent of Babtel owned by my children Chris, Luke, Megan and Peter. USA-BROAD is raising $12 million through the EB-5 program. Half of that money will be used to buy out all the other shareholders in BATEL. After the EB-5 money is raised, Babtel will be 100 percent owned by USABROAD.

But in 2012, I went back to the board, and I said I wanted to pay back the old investors and asked for a plan to do so.

One of the board members asked, "Didn't you start a company, and everybody lost their money?"

"Why? What's the big deal? It's just money," I said.

"You didn't have a pot to piss in. You were flat on your back in a prison cell. Nobody paid any attention to you. They cast you aside. You lost all of our money. Now you've made all of the money back, and you want to pay us back, and you're asking what's the big deal?"

The reality is, there is no big deal. Money is just numbers on a piece of paper, and it's entirely irrelevant to me. What does matter to me is that the guys who were with me in the Iraq War stuck it out with me and we didn't get crushed. We didn't get destroyed (but we almost did) and we came back stronger than ever. That's the way life is, so that's the way we run our company. That's what relationships and this business is all about. We're willing to stick together through the tough times and still have a good time during it all.

As you can see, the ego in the case of the tech boom was the death of me. It was the death of the company. It cost everybody their jobs. It caused much turmoil in many people's lives because I had no way of getting past my ego at that particular moment in my life. Now my ego's still there. It's just taken a different form, and I don't take it so seriously. I see the split brain, I see my split mind, and I realize it's my ego. I know I still have my inner voice. I didn't even know I had an inner voice until I was in jail in Lebanon. Fortunately, I ended up there at that place in my life as I don't know if I'd ever have been quiet enough to hear it.

This approach of feeling safe enough to fail can make life hap-hazard as the ups and downs can be quite unstable. There's something to be said for stability and safety, and our approach is not what you'd call safe. It might only be good for our business because we work in war zones, so the nature of our work is quite risky. Taking risks and feeling safe enough to fail might not be the way that everybody wants to live, but it's the way that we've gone.

I've always felt that if you're not hot or you're not cold, you're playing it safe. I can't do it. I can't live any other way than I do, but the way that I've chosen to live my life isn't something that I'd force on anyone else. It's fun, and we make money, but there's a cost. That's why we don't get angry with people for failing in what we do; we love each other more as a result of it. We encourage each other as we know that failure happens to all of us. We can get hurt because we take risks, so we laugh about it, and don't take it that seriously. I understand that this lifestyle isn't for everybody. Perhaps it's better for some people to play it safe, take a 9-5 job, save for retirement, don't take any significant risks and budget yourself; perhaps some people need to be stable and safe and secure. While there's something to be said for that, I can't do it — I never could.

I'm describing very uncomfortable circumstances long after they happened. I've always said to my children that all adventure is in discomfort remembered. When we're talking about getting shot down in helicopters, being kidnapped, and getting thrown in prisons, most people don't consider such events to be fun. I see what I want to see and I misinterpret everything that happens, and I don't think I'm any different from anybody else in that way.

Allowing our people to feel safe enough to fail comes from a heart that understands that our work is dangerous. We fail all the time as it's the nature of our business. We put our focus on staying alive and helping each other make it through. For me, there's no such thing as making a mistake. I don't know anyone I've ever met who didn't make mistakes. I'm able to forgive myself for all the mistakes I make, and that drives people crazy. I make all kinds of stupid harebrained mistakes, and I've done so all my life. I look back and see I was stupid to do certain things. It hasn't, however, stopped me from making a different mistake down the line. Why? Because I feel safe enough to fail.

CHAPTER SIX

GIVE GUIDANCE AND HELP WITH HUMILITY AND THOUGHTFULNESS.

Give guidance and help with humility and thoughtfulness. A good manager knows when to withhold guidance (for example, when it makes a person feel foolish and inadequate) and when to offer it gently (for example, when a person asks for it or is too lost to know what to ask for). Although we won't take our staff's power or autonomy away, we will offer to do some of the more challenging parts of their jobs when needed. This is a careful dance that we all must do when we manage other people. We need to recognize the areas in which our teams feel most vulnerable and incapable and need to offer the right kind of help without shaming them with humility.

I'm the first to admit that our business philosophy could be challenging for a traditional corporate executive to embrace but it's entirely possible. For example, I've been friends with Paul Johnson — vice president and co-founder of Globecomm Systems for more than 20 years — and he's currently the CEO of Babtel. Even though Paul is what you'd consider corporate, he hopped in a taxi with me and rode from Baghdad to Joint Base Balad in the middle of a war. He has a corporate side, but even though he's never been in trouble and he's careful about everything he does, when it gets right down to it, there's no stopping him.

The company Paul founded with a few other friends of mine from New York had one of the most wonderful satellite companies with which I've ever worked, Globecomm Systems. When I walked in there, I was like a kid in a candy store. The technology they were working on for people all over the world was so impressive. They took a liking to us and incubated one of the first startups I mentioned earlier, Skyway Partners.

Globecomm Systems had incubated Skyway Partners and had given us office space and tons of equipment when we were building, and they gave us one of their board of directors to be on our board. They added credence to our company, which helped us get going with Skyway at the time. They helped by introducing us to Bob Towbin, of C.E Unterberg, Towbin & Co., who was on the board of Globecomm Systems. Bob was the underwriter who raised the $5 million for us, which was incredibly helpful. As I mentioned, however, during the tech crash, we lost Skyway Partners.

I want to illustrate how Paul was able to give guidance with humility and thoughtfulness by telling the story about how this seemingly corporate guy was able to operate in the real world. He got me out of a big jam that I was in with our

Lebanese bandwidth provider. They were having a tough time giving us satellite bandwidth at Joint Base Balad, and we were going down about 15 times a day. Every time the network went down, we would have to spend hours re-aligning all of our access points on the base.

Paul's company, Globecomm Systems, was also a satellite company and so when I told him about the problems I was having, he said, "Cancel your contract with them, and we'll take over." He offered to do the site survey himself. So he flew to Iraq, brought an engineer with him, and we traveled about 100 miles by road through four or five hazardous areas where there were known Al-Qaeda cells. He was so fearless. I thought perhaps he was an ex-Marine. I didn't know him that well at that time, but that's when we started to work closely together.

Globecomm was able to get our bandwidth fixed, and help us get that network on its feet at that particular point. We'd been struggling for more than a year, and it had been a disaster. Incidentally, it was primarily because of that move away from the Lebanese investors to Globecomm that had me arrested and thrown in jail. The Lebanese were still mad about me kicking them off the base.

When Globecomm was sold, Paul was free, but he had a non-compete clause. We couldn't hire Paul right then, but as soon as he was off his non-compete, we asked him to become CEO of Babtel. He's an anomaly in the corporate world as he knows how to dot all the *i*s and cross all the *t*s, and not take any unnecessary risk, but at the same time, he'll get in a taxi and drive with you across a war zone while you're being fired upon. He's corporate, yet a risk taker at the same time; that's a combination you don't often see. Globecomm was a publicly traded company, and if anything had happened to Paul while he was in Iraq with me, the company could have been sued by his estate, and it would have driven the company into complete and utter ruin.

Globecomm took a huge risk on me to start Babtel even more than usual because they had public money behind them. A mishap could have resulted in all kinds of lawsuits and possibly even criminal litigation — many things that happen in a public company that don't happen in a private company. People can claim all kinds of things and can sue you for a ham sandwich in this country. If you send people into dangerous areas as a publicly traded company, you're risking the money of your public investors, and there are rules against that.

In 2015, we were in the process of building out a contract; we'd got this massive contract at CENTCOM headquarters in Qatar. After I was released from prison in Lebanon and was thrown out of the company by my son, and my wife left me, I ended up in Afghanistan doing what I called Rent-a-Jackass, which was never really a business. When I left jail, I didn't have anything, except USABROAD, and since we didn't have any business, I called some friends and said, "Hey, I'm down on my luck. If you need anybody to do site surveys or put deals together or do quotes for you out in the middle of any of those dangerous countries, you can hire me to do it." They started laughing, and many of them said, "You're a jackass." That's why I decided to call the service Rent-a-Jackass.

While I was doing Rent-a-Jackass, I discovered this technology that was being used by some smart Canadians who had started a company called Leaky Coax. It involved a GSM architecture that they'd adapted to be used for Wi-Fi for regular Internet in military operations, and it worked well. The technology would have saved us millions of dollars had we known about it a few years before when we were in Iraq.

Primarily, it was a coax cable with holes in it which you could use to broadcast into challenging areas, such as mine shafts and containerized housing units which are entirely covered with metal. When attempting to transmit Wi-Fi signals into those areas, it ricochets and bounces around. With Leaky Coax cable, you could drill a hole through the building, run the wire through it and leak the signal into the building inside of trying to penetrate it with Wi-Fi frequencies from outside of the building.

When I saw it, I knew it was a multimillion-dollar idea, so I brought it to Qatar, and it caught on. The military loved it and started to use my company for doing all their projects, and I ended up getting some significant bases. Eventually, we ended up with this huge base called Al-Udeid Air Base in 2014, as we signed the contract in December 2014 and then we started building it in 2015.

When I was in Afghanistan, I'd taken money from people, and made commitments that if I signed any more deals down in Qatar, I'd make this particular man the project manager. He was a former captain in the air force. I knew that I was getting close to this Al-Udeid job, and I needed somebody to go over there and do the project management work. I didn't think it was a big deal, as he seemed like a nice guy and had $75,000 to put into the company, and I needed $75,000 at the time. He invested in USABROAD, and as soon as I got the contract, I made him the project manager.

Well, he went to the base and fell flat on his face, and it became clear that he'd never led a project before. He was making all kinds of mistakes. He'd get up late at 10 a.m. He'd forget their tools. He'd never stage their equipment on time. He never had an installation plan. He didn't know what he was doing at all.

I don't know how to run a project, but my son Peter does, and he's a sound technician. When we had our troubles in Iraq, and we went out of business, Peter left the company too, leaving his brother to run it. Peter took a job with a company in the Philadelphia area called Brandywine Technologies, and during two years he learned everything about project management that he could learn. He got several certifications for Wi-Fi technologies, for Cisco technologies mostly, and he came out of there a completely changed person. When he came back to work for the company (and I was doing the Rent-a-Jackass thing), we started working together again.

After I got those contracts, he came back full-time. I said to Peter, "Look, we're having a problem at Al-Udeid, we've got a guy in there, and the only thing he does is worry about what people think about him. He's not thinking about getting the job done. He's not thinking about the people that are doing the job. He worries about how he looks in front of everybody.

It's not going over well, it's coming across in a negative way, nobody likes him, and the thing's falling apart. We need to get this thing back on its wheels again."

Peter flew to the base at Qatar to check out the situation. The first thing he did was give me a list of tools to buy, and said, "Get off the base and away from this operation. The more involved you are, the worse it gets, because the more you confront this manager about how he's missing the mark, the more defensive he's getting. Get a hotel someplace and don't show up. I'll give you jobs to do, and then you do what I tell you to do until this situation is under control."

I listened to what he told me to do, and I got a hotel room and bought the equipment he told me to get. Then he took over the job as project manager. Instead of telling people what to do, he packed up everything in the morning, put together an installation schedule, and went out on the installation schedule, bringing this other guy with him.

He would ask the guy, "What do you think about this? How do you think we should handle that?" Even though the guy didn't know what he was doing, Peter would suggest, "How about doing it this way?" or "How about doing it that way?" Little by little, Peter, in his way, taught this guy exactly what he had to do to run the project. Peter spent two months with the guy and got the guy on his feet and showed him what had to be done.

The guy had never run a project before; he didn't know that much about Wi-Fi. He was a desktop management guy for Internet services for certain branches of the military that had those secure Internet connections. All he did was handle their email and Internet. He didn't have any idea about infrastructure, so Peter had to teach it to him. The guy learned it, and he was happy to learn it. He got the project on track, and everything was going fine. Peter's way of handling the whole situation, however, was so pleasant and a real lesson to me. Peter did not go in there as a 900 lb. gorilla to fix everything. He went in there like a servant to show those guys that he wasn't above punching down cables, running wires, or getting dirty. He wasn't above any of the menial jobs there were to do.

He didn't boss anybody around. Instead, he did what had to be done, taking it one step at a time, and showing the guy how to build a network. In this loving, gentle and thoughtful way, Peter taught the guy everything he didn't know in just two months. We got the network up and running, and everything was excellent, and right after we got the system running, the guy quit. At least, though, he got us through the installation phase. Peter was able to guide with humility and thoughtfulness. Sometimes you have to step up, and sometimes you have to do it quietly. And sometimes, as it was for me, you have to get in the back seat, and let someone else run the show.

At present, we've a new contract in Qatar to provide the overall telecommunications services for a small army base called Camp As Sayliyah. I hired a guy almost a year ago to take over for me in this area doing business development. He was assigned this contract and took it over while we handled the technology for him, and he took care of all the relationships. This particular contract is being administered differently from other deals we have because it's going through a payment system at the base called wide-area workflow (WAWF). The air force and army have adopted WAWF as a new automated financial payment system. We don't use it under contracts except for this one.

Although this contract has been going out for five months now, we hadn't been paid. We had to make significant payments to local carriers in Qatar, such as the telephone company Ooredoo, which were demanding money. We hadn't been getting any money from this project because of a new payment system, and the numbers had gotten pretty big. It was more than a quarter of a million dollars of back payments. In the meantime, we were paying all those bills for the other telecommunications carriers out of our pocket.

We couldn't get the money, yet this guy was doing everything he possibly could. I knew in my heart of hearts that he had this thing in a graveyard spin. It was entirely out of control. Every day he was calling this guy, calling that guy, flying here, flying there, to Kuwait, to Qatar. He was working on this problem day in, day out, going to everybody, and beating on their desk. The more that he pushed and the more that he tried to get it done, the more screwed up it got, and this went on for months.

Finally, the corporate guy called me and said, "Chris, don't you think it's about time you start to escalate this to the next level? You must get this in front of CENTCOM because if you don't get this in front of CENTCOM, we're going to suffer serious financial consequences."

"He has this thing under control," I assured him.

"He's been working on it for five months, he hasn't gotten any money out of these people, and we have to pay this next bill right now!"

It was a Monday, and we owed them another $50,000 within a few days.

I said, "He has it under control. Let's give him a chance to let it happen."

He said, "Okay. It's your call."

On Friday, we got paid, and then we were able to make the payment on Monday as required. It would, however, have been a lot easier if I had acted out of fear, and stepped in and taken over, escalated it to the next level, and sent somebody to bounce on somebody else's desk to make it happen. That might have made it worse. I don't know.

Following our strategy of not stealing the power from people who work for us, and being willing to take a risk with them, we waited. My guy said to me later, "I knew this was totally out of control. I'd done everything I could to make it happen. I talked to everybody; I went everywhere I could go. Then we had a president who died, and then another holiday for another two nights. I finally let go. With just two days before the next crisis point, there was nothing more that I could do other than what I was already doing, so I dropped it. I followed your strategy of the graveyard spin, took my hands off the helm, and waited to see if everything would come back together."

He listened to his heart, and as soon as he let go, we got paid. The money somehow trickled through the system, and we got the first payment of $92,000, so we were able to pay our bills. We were paid ahead of time, and we were able to pay our bills as soon as he finally let go. He later shared with me that he knew he was in a graveyard spin, so he knew to let go and let it happen.

If I encounter people who exhibit other traits — perhaps the opposite of humility — that doesn't make any difference to me. We're all the same, and we have both sides. The only difference between somebody who's not listening and somebody who is listening to their inner voice is that they forgot they have an inner voice. No one would choose not to listen to his or her inner voice if he or she knew they had one. Most people have forgotten.

You never know what life's going to bring you, and you've got to keep your eyes open to whatever life brings you because that could be the next person that's going to be able to be the most help. You have to keep the options open and keep your mind open. Just because somebody comes as a completely self-centered person, he could be the closest person ever to finding his inner voice.

My people work under harsh conditions. They work during war, and they've seen and experienced things the average person does not. If they have trouble, we try and get them home as fast as we can to be with their families and extended family systems in which they get some emotional support. We make sure that we take care of them and we stick with them until they're ready to come back.

Most of the people who work for us are other country nationals, and there often aren't resources like counseling in most of the countries where they live (Nepal and the Philippines, for example). Counseling is hard to appreciate as a concept for countries where life and death are always close, and people are often on the brink of survival. They're on the verge of extinction in some cases. The places where most of my people come from are difficult in general, and the idea of going to a counselor because you're in a challenging circumstance is a little bit outside the box for them.

The majority of the people who work with me would probably say that counseling creates imaginary solutions for nonexistent problems. When you're under fire, and you have all kinds of difficulties hitting you, you've a fear that continually batters you and your fears become your reality. This has also happened to me. You feel fear, and you're on edge, and this can make you more manipulative and controlling, and can make you have all the other behaviors that go along with fear. If this happens in everybody's normal life, it's multiplied in a war environment.

The only way to unwind it is to climb up the same ladder that you climbed down to get into it. What you need is to get back into your partner's arms, or hold your little child. You need to get reconnected with love and the things in the world that are so wonderful. All the other things that we pay experts for will shade in comparison with getting connected again with your family.

Fortunately, in most of the countries my people come from, there are incredible extended family systems in which people are supportive and loving and caring. It's not like in America, where you come home, and you have a nuclear family, and maybe a divorce, and people are split up, and they don't have any support, and must pay a counselor to listen to them. If it wasn't for my wife and her love and support for me when I went through some of the stuff that I went through, I don't know how I'd ever have been able to reconnect to reality.

It doesn't always take a spouse. It could be parents, siblings, friends or any extended family system that gives people emotional support. Those inner connections bring us naturally back to being a human again instead of doing it artificially through some psychological gymnastics or prescriptions or medication. Relationships are the most healing thing. That's why when you go to countries such as Iraq where they've been doing nothing but fighting wars for years, those people are amazingly productive and healthy for what they go through daily. Some of these people have known nothing but war their whole life.

They get married, and they have children, and they do everything that ordinary people do amid all the calamities they're undergoing; the pain and the suffering and the hunger and the trauma, and getting shot at all the time. It's difficult for me to think that I'm setting an example of how to guide with humility and thoughtfulness during difficult times compared to what those guys go through on an average day. More often than not, I'm learning from them.

CHAPTER SEVEN

CREATE A CONTAINER FOR COMPLEX EMOTIONS, FEAR, TRAUMA, ETC.

Create a container for complex emotions, fear, trauma, etc. Especially when we deploy people in non-permissive environments when we follow the above practices, people feel that they are held in a deeper way than they are used to. They feel safe enough to allow complex emotions to surface that might normally remain hidden. We need to be aware that this can happen and be prepared to accept the situation in gentle, supportive and nonjudgmental ways. We need to be an example of a place where people feel safe enough to fall apart without fearing that this will leave them permanently broken or that others will shame them on a project. We must always be there to offer strength and courage. This isn't easy work, and it's work that we all continue to learn about as we face more challenging situations increasingly. We cannot do it if we are overly emotional ourselves, if we haven't done the hard work of looking into our own shadow, or if we don't trust the people we are working with. In such situations, we'll do our best to show all teams tenderness, compassion and confidence.

During my time in Iraq, there was a hotel in Baghdad called the Al-Hamra Hotel. All the news people used to gather there to write their articles, and communicate with the press corps back home. I used to hang out there too because I liked to find out what was going on, and I could find people to help me.

I needed a driver and someone to help to get through the war, as I was alone at that point. I had already started Babtel, and we had some customers. I was working for security companies in Baghdad who were communicating with outside vendors to provide armored cars, body armor and ammunition. They needed telecommunications to do so, and I provided their telecom.

In search of a driver, I went to Al-Hamra and put the word out that I needed a driver. Soon they sent over a guy called Firaz, who came with high recommendations. He was a Sunni from Ramadi, which was right next to Fallujah, the real center for the mujahideen and the resistance. He spoke a dialect of Arabic only used in that one area.

I hired him, and my new friend and I hit it off right away. He thought I was the craziest guy he'd ever met in his life for being in Iraq and living on the local economy in downtown Baghdad. I thought he was mad too because he was working for the press corps and his life was in danger every single day. He took reporters to meetings with Iraqi chiefs and sheikhs around town who told the reporters what was happening from their perspective, so we were both in high-risk situations.

Firaz brought me to a translator in town who made Arabic cards for me. I started memorizing Arabic words and was able to speak with him in broken Arabic, while he tried to communicate with me in broken English. Over a period of two or three years, we were able to communicate quite well. Eventually, he said he needed to protect me by coming up with some cover story for me living in the local economy in case I got kidnapped.

Firaz's father had been a general in the air force under Saddam Hussein, and he ran the air force academy under Saddam for a long time before he retired. My cover story was necessary in case I got picked up, so he suggested we pick a name from the mujahideen area of Iraq so that people would be afraid of me. They chose the name Sultan Al-Dulaimy. Al-Dulaimy was the most prominent mujahideen family in Iraq, and Sultan means king. They were related to my friend's father. In case I got tripped up, I was to say that I was connected to them and that Firaz was my cousin.

Sure enough, I was kidnapped by Al-Qaeda in the southern part of Iraq. The police held me while I was being brokered into an Al-Qaeda cell. They ultimately planned to execute me.

Firaz was with me when I was picked up, so he called his father, and his father called the police department and said, "I want you to release our cousin."

They asked, "What do you mean your cousin?"

"Our cousin Sultan Al-Dulaimy grew up in America. When he was a child, the Saddam regime executed his parents, and he was adopted by a Greek family who emigrated to America. Now that Iraq is free from Saddam, he's come back to re-establish his connections with his family, and he's staying with us in Iraq. I want you to release our cousin."

They said, "No. We're going to sell your cousin to one of these cells for $10,000, and then we'll split the money with you."

Firaz's father said, "You release our cousin today, or by tomorrow morning at this time, everyone in your police department will be dead, including you."

Two hours later, I was free, and so I owed my life to Firaz and his father.

A few years after this happened, Firaz came into my office, crying.

He said, "On my way to the airport today, we were going too fast through a checkpoint. A private first class opened fire on us and shot my son through the head." His son Mustafa was just two years old at this point.

"Have you seen Mustafa?" I asked.

"No, we can't see him because he's held in Jaysh al-Mahdi territory."

This was the Shiite militia group that was protecting that part of Baghdad. They had the toddler and were holding him in a hospital there, knowing that Firaz's father, who was a well-known Sunni patriarch, would come to see his grandson and they would have the opportunity to grab him and kill him. In other words, this was a complete disaster.

I asked, "How much money do we have in the cash box?"

"About $300," Firaz said.

I was already putting on my boots, wondering what we were going to do, and I said aloud, "We're going to get Mustafa." (Christopher is translated to Mustafa in Arabic, so Firaz had named his son after me.)

As per our company policy, I knew I had to offer strength and courage. It wasn't unusual to face challenging situations, as every day we operated in a war zone. I knew I could not be overly emotional, and that I had to show tenderness, compassion and confidence. I also knew, however, that I was probably going to do something perilous to get the little boy out of the hospital. Moreover, even if we got him out, we had no idea about the seriousness of his condition. I felt we had no other choice but to do our best to rescue him.

Understandably, Firaz was very upset about the entire situation. He didn't think there was any hope, and he was on the brink of a breakdown. I loved Mustafa too, and I'd known him since he was born. As per the Iraqi tradition, when family comes over, they put money in the baby basket that the baby's sleeping in, I had put $100 in his crib. I'd been close to him since he was born, and of course, I didn't want him to die.

We took the car and raced across Baghdad to the hospital in the Jaysh al-Mahdi territory. We parked the car, walked inside, and found the room where the little boy was being held. I told Firaz to go outside and back up the car to the door and wait for me. As soon as I came out with his son, he was to hit the gas, and we would get the hell out of there. My friend did as I asked. I took all the money I had, which was $300 in twenties and fifties, and handed out bills to each of the people on the floor, asking a nurse to remove the IV from Mustafa's arm.

I scooped the little guy up in my arms and ran out the back door with him clutched to my chest, jumping in the back seat of the car as Firaz put the pedal to the floor. We broke through the gate, and Firaz raced the car down backstreets toward the Green Zone to bring his son to the American hospital. We were chased the entire way across the city, and although we were being fired upon, we made it. When we got to the Green Zone, they let us in, and we took the boy to the hospital and told them that an American soldier had shot him. They rushed Mustafa to Joint Base Balad where they performed emergency brain surgery on him. The boy made a complete recovery, and is now living a normal life. The United States government gave the family a $100,000 settlement, which is a lot of money for an Iraqi. The settlement changed things for their family.

While way off the spectrum of what most business people might address in their career, this story is a perfect example of how I had to keep my cool in a situation and do what was necessary to provide leadership for Firaz. To be clear, it's not that I wasn't afraid. I was aware that the three of us could be killed. Saving the boy, however, was the only choice that I thought we had given those circumstances. I had to listen to my heart and my inner voice instead of my ego.

I felt that I owed my life to their family, as they'd saved me from certain execution. As far as I was concerned, I was on borrowed time as it was. When I learned about Mustafa's situation, I knew what I needed to do, and I did it. I maintained the container of my emotions, and kept control over my fear, and was able to deal with the circumstances and do what had to be done, and it worked. I'm so grateful, as things could have gone the other way.

While many of these stories can be interchangeable according to how we relate each one of the eight principles in many ways, this story is a perfect demonstration of how I had to construct a container for my feelings to continue to function. There wasn't much room for error in the case of Firaz and Mustafa.

CHAPTER EIGHT

ALLOW THEM TO MAKE DIFFERENT DECISIONS AND HAVE DIFFERENT EXPERIENCES FROM YOUR OWN.

Allow them to make different decisions and to have different experiences from your own. In large part, managing effectively involves respecting each person's differences and recognizing that those differences may lead to other people making choices that we wouldn't make. Sometimes, for example, they make choices based on cultural norms that we can't understand from within our own experience. When we accept people's diversity, we release, and we honor differences.

Every time we get into a situation where we're encouraging other people to express their opinions, naturally they're going to come up with their views. If you've given your teams the authority to make decisions — which you must do so you don't steal their power — you also must trust their choices.

In the course of business dealings, every leader is going to face a variety of industry-specific decisions and challenges. If people don't feel empowered to operate without your direct input, a variety of situations could occur. People could worry they won't get what they need, so they find a way to take it from someone else. They may go in the wrong direction and feel miserable, because they're so far down the ladder as victims that they feel like failures.

Perhaps they pass the buck and blame everybody else instead of taking responsibility for themselves. If they don't see themselves as a valuable part in the collective whole of the company, your people won't have the tools to make any decisions, let alone those that may be different from what you would have chosen.

For example, we recently had a problem in one of our Qatar locations. Our Internet started dropping every 15 minutes. One of the technicians realized that the trouble with the Internet began after a firmware upgrade, so he took it upon himself to make a decision. He thought if he changed the channel width from 200 to 400 megahertz, people would not be knocked off the Internet. He came up with the idea, and when people see precisely what they want to see, they misinterpret the results, so he thought it was working.

There are only three non-overlapping channels on a Wi-Fi network on that frequency of 2.4 gigs. It's 1, 6 and 11, but you need to maintain the channel width at 200 megahertz for each channel. Every technician knows this, but this guy didn't. We lost our channel space on Channels 1, 3 and 6, and that's why nobody could stay on the Internet. Our sales plummeted, and we went from $10,000 a day to $6,000 a day.

People were coming up with a variety of different reasons for what might have happened to cause the problem. While the technician had created the problem, he didn't tell anybody that he tried to fix the other problem. Since he didn't document his intervention, there was no way that we could go through the network logs, and see what went awry. He made a mistake, never documented his error, and broke all the standard rules in the process of running a network.

When you want to make a change in a network, you first discuss it with your peers, and then you test the difference in a limited environment. You don't roll it out until it's agreed by all that it works. After you and the team understand that it works, then you roll it out globally but do it gradually. You make sure to document it and observe it so that you don't make a major blunder and affect the entire network.

This technician did everything wrong that he could do wrong. Then he tried to cover it up because he didn't want to get fired. Finally, my son got involved and noticed the network configurations and saw that somebody had made the change from 200 to 400 megahertz. He noticed the date and time it took place. He identified the guy who was on duty at that particular time and called him.

The guy admitted to having made the change, and we immediately corrected it. As soon as we fixed it, the problems abated. In fact, in about three days, we had gone from 60 service calls a day to three. It was an artificial problem that didn't exist because we had a firmware upgrade that naturally led to some disruption in the network. The technician caused significant disruption for all of our customers and our bottom line; we lost $5,000 a day for two weeks straight.

Rather than fire the guy, we used the lesson to help everyone else on the team. We pointed out that it's vital to respect each other enough to talk about decisions that we think we should make. We highlighted why it's essential that we follow documentation procedures as a team, and not go off on our own and do what we want to do to fix it. I didn't bring up the fact that this technician covered up his mistake, but only emphasized the positive. It was a good thing for all of us to learn in that particular environment; you can't change a 2.4 gig network from 200 to 400 megahertz and expect that it's going to work.

If we have one of these tiny, mad ideas inside of us and it's going to manifest itself into a significant problem, that could disrupt the workplace. It doesn't matter if it works. It's going to make us feel like a special person because we came up with a solution to this issue. That's not what we're after; we're after making sure that we respect each other. We care about our customers. We care about their experience in communicating with their loved ones back home, and we put that above our desire to try and solve a problem, and feel right about our idea, and feel special about solving something.

To the team, we emphasized the need to see this occurrence as a way in which we can screw up our customers and our company by not caring enough about each other. If we care about our customer, we care about each other, and we're not going to make mistakes like that. We're going to talk about them with each other before we pull the trigger. That's the thing that we took away from it. I thanked this technician for his great job and said that it was an excellent lesson for all of us.

The more significant issue is not that we lost $5,000 a day while the network was down. It was more important that I was able to provide a valuable illustration of why we need to care about our customers and care about and respect each other. When you trust other people to make decisions that are different from yours, you then you don't want to be punishing them when they make mistakes. Situations will come up in life that look punishable by usual, corporate standards. If, however, you punish people, you're going to exacerbate the problem of people trying to cover up mistakes and hide them, instead of celebrating what's right in the lessons learned.

If we celebrate our mistakes and the things that we do wrong in a constructive way, we move forward. If we don't listen to our inner voice and how we deal with these circumstances, we end up stepping on people, making them feel bad, or even worse, hurting them and their families. That creates a toxic environment and is the worst thing to do. Even though this occurrence I'm discussing affected other people, and even though it hurt other people, when you're talking about the Internet, what's the worst that's going to happen? Somebody's not going to get Internet for a few days. It's not a life-and-death situation.

It wasn't a great idea to do what he did, but it wasn't a devastating problem either. I've made worse mistakes. For example, one time in Iraq, our network was having trouble, and my solution to everything back in those days was to reboot. Well, I pulled the power switch to the whole network and shut the entire building down. Then I flipped it back the other way, and when I did that, I caused so many problems.

There was a $250,000 earth station we had that was tracking a Turkish elliptical-orbit satellite each 100th of a degree. Every time it went out of orbit a 100th of a degree, it would move a little bit. We lost the whole tracking program when I did this. My son Peter had to stay up all night and the next day, and my son Luke took the shift after that. My sons spent a total of 48 hours reestablishing this program, then they said to me, "Dad, if you ever walk into our network operation center again, we're both going home." I've respected their words, and I don't mess around with their world anymore. Now I focus on sales and raising money, and I let them handle the technology.

I accept the fact that we're going to make mistakes, and we're going to have differences. I celebrate the diversity that we have with each other, and look at life, and look at our relationship, and look at our company as a classroom, where we're all learning at every level. I've often noticed that children know how to celebrate diversity, while adults can forget. We must remember that everyone's a student in this classroom called life, and as problems arise, how we deal with them are the lessons we learn. You're either following the egoistic sense of specialness, authority and individuality, or you're following the inner voice of building unity, peace, love and joy.

In this chapter dealing with the importance of allowing our people to make different decisions from our own, I've just recounted one example of a smaller error or judgment and how as a team we were quickly able to remedy the problem. Next, I'll discuss a more complicated case. Because I'm working with the military, I hire those with a military mentality, and the way the military thinks is generally not the way I think.

The military has a strict way of doing things, and when people screw up, they get court-martialed. If they screw up in the line of duty, and they're in a deployed, non-permissive environment, people could get seriously hurt. There's not much room for a mishap in that world, as it's a dangerous environment in which they live. Although I'm right beside them, we function differently, and that can be a challenge.

We're not on the ground, and we're not facing enemies with weapons. Our typical hire faces the same kind of hardship that the majority of the troops face — not the troops who are the ground pounders or special service or the marines or the infantry, but most of the logistics people who do the support work. We face the same dangers. We are similar to a paramilitary logistics group; we're next to and alongside them.

I hire people from the military to run our company so that they will get along with the military guys we work alongside. They have to fit into this entirely different world in the way we do things. Not only is it difficult for them, but it's always a real learning experience for me. The failures are so dramatic that frequently I wonder how there can be two worlds that are so different and so far apart, yet so close together while living and working.

An essential part of this story is that I came to notice a pattern in hiring from the military. When certain men progress up the military organization to a certain point, they may discover that they don't have what it takes to get past a particular rank. While some are perfectly happy at lieutenant colonel, some get their feelings hurt because they won't make colonel. If they're passed over a few times, they become more egoistic instead of accepting the fact that it just wasn't the place for them. They take it personally as if a lieutenant colonel gets passed over twice, that's the end of his career. They immediately have to leave, because once you're passed over twice, you never make it to the next rank.

It doesn't matter which rank we hire from, but we have to be careful when we hire ex-military once they've been passed over a few times. They could have a lot of hard feelings about their position, especially in a military organization. In this next story, this is precisely what happened as a man we hired had moved right along to lieutenant colonel, but he was not promoted to colonel. You won't get to the next rank if you've reached your maximum capability of leadership at the point where you're so egoistic that you can't move forward. Life will stop you right there. The hiring of a lieutenant colonel was the biggest failure I ever had in trying to teach these eight principles to a new member of our team.

Back in 2015, I was doing a build-out in Qatar. It was a big one; perhaps the biggest one that we've done since the Iraq war. We were on a large base with 10,000 guys, with about a $5 million capital-expenditure build. A critical side story is that at this time I was experiencing a strange paralysis on the left side of my body that came and went several times per day. I went to the clinic on base, where the doctor told me, "You probably have a pinched nerve. Have it looked at when you go back to the States." Since I didn't have covered medical treatment on base, he couldn't treat me, but only offer friendly advice.

We finished the build, and I went back to the States about six months later.

My doctor examined me and said, "I don't believe your symptoms are a result of a pinched nerve because it's happening from the top of your head to the tip of your toe. If it were just a pinched nerve, it would stop at your neck. You'd better go in for an MRI."

I had an MRI, and when I was seen by the head of a neurology department back in Pennsylvania, I was told, "You've got a serious problem. It looks like you have an incurable, terminal condition, and you may not have more than 90 days to live."

I said, "What? I feel fine!"

He said, "You've had over 200 TIA (transient ischemic attack) strokes. When you have a TIA, the flow of blood to part of your brain gets cut off for a short time. A TIA can be a sign that a full-blown stroke is on the way. TIAs are short and won't cause lasting damage, but it's important to treat them like an emergency and get care right away. You've also had five full-blown killer strokes, and we have no idea how you are walking, talking, or functioning. We don't think that you have much time in this world. You'd better get your things in order."

"Don't you think you need a second opinion?" I asked, aghast.

"We already have one from Johns Hopkins. They agree with us."

"Isn't there a way to put in a stent?" I asked after learning I had two blocked carotid arteries on my right side, and no blood had been getting to the right side of my brain for years.

That explained why I had lost my creativity and ability to feel emotion, as I mentioned in an earlier chapter. I hadn't been able to process fear, anxiety or other negative emotions, but it was a grave condition, nonetheless.

Stunned, I talked to my son and my daughter about my prognosis. I spoke to my chief financial officer at the time, and she felt so sad about it that she decided to leave. She'd been a good friend of mine for 20 years, and she couldn't take it, so she went. My son Peter and I agreed that we had to find a replacement for me.

I said, "I don't want you continually traveling around the world and having the same kinds of problems with your family as I've had with mine. Stay at home with your wife and raise your family, but hire people to do what I do. Don't do the traveling and take risks. Many people can do it, and you don't have to put yourself in the way of harm."

Peter had spent six years in Iraq getting shot at, so he didn't have any problem going into harm's way, but God forbid something should happen to him. He's the technical brains of the company and has helped advance us technically in many ways. We cannot risk him.

We put out the word that we wanted to hire a senior military officer to take over my role in the company, and soon found a retired lieutenant colonel from the army's special forces. We brought him into the company and briefed him on the eight points. I had him write his contract, so before he came on board full-time, we worked for six months developing his contract, plan and strategy for his takeover. He was the most excited and gung-ho person in the world until he started working.

Since he spoke fluent Chinese, he was supposed to be supporting my Chinese operation. It wasn't a military operation, but an investment project to raise money through the investor immigration program called EB-5. Much money comes into the United States through Chinese investors in this program, and I wanted him to develop that arm of the company. He was primed to raise money and do sales work, which is what I do.

I wanted him to head to central command in the Middle East and witness how the eight points that were in his contract were facilitated. When he got over there, he saw that that military operation was so mature that he wanted to be a part of that instead. He completely ignored just about everything else we had asked him to do with the EB-5 program and focused only on going to our bases that do nothing but serve the soldiers. He wanted to be with the troops as that was his environment, and he felt comfortable with them.

As a lieutenant colonel, when he fell back into that environment, he also fell back into his old ways of thinking, which is contrary to the way we run our operation. He was condescending to our people, he was bullying, and he threatened to fire people. He had no power to fire people, however, as we have a no-firing policy in our company, yet he was horrible to people. He made members of staff cry.

Finally, I had to pull him out of there. I said, "I don't want you to go back there. If you can't control yourself and follow the principles you agreed to in your contract, you're of no use to me." Well, it was horrible for him to hear that and it hurt his feelings so deeply that he never spoke to me again. He went to my children, to my board and to everybody else in my company and told them that I had to leave. He said that I was insane and that I didn't know what I was doing. He said that I was ruining the company; the very company I had built. He also said that I wasn't fit to run a hot-dog stand. Well, he's right about that one.

I had to do the same thing with him that I would've done with anybody else; I had to follow my eight points. I listened to and accepted what he said, then said to him, "I believe that you believe what you're claiming, and I don't agree with you. However, this is what you signed up to do, and if you can't do that, you have to learn how to do so." He treated the issue as though it was just a transitional problem. I said, "I know you're in a transition to a new way of thinking and I will not lose faith that you will come around."

A side story is that after that year of thinking I was going to die, my daughter said she thought I should consult another doctor or investigate another form of medicine. She brought me to an Indian doctor who practiced Ayurvedic medicine.

The doctor said to me, "You're a mess. Your liver's a disaster. Your circulation is horrible. What's going on with you?"

I told her I was dying, and she said I was not.

I said, "Well, I am. Western medical professionals have told me that my time is up."

She asked, "How long ago were you supposed to die?"

"90 days."

She asked me how long ago that was, and I told her it was more than a year.

"I guess they were wrong," she said.

I told her I didn't believe they were wrong; maybe they'd made a miscalculation.

"Chris, the human being is a lot more than just a body; the human being is an embodied spirit," she explained. "And if your spirit isn't ready to die, it can drag your body along for quite some time. We know this in our type of business. They don't teach this way of thinking in Western medicine, but they teach this in Eastern medicine."

She went on to say, "Your spirit is fine, and you're full of life. We can turn your physical body around in about four months." Well, this was a vastly different story from what my Western doctors told me. When I asked what to do, she said, "Get some sleep at night. In the morning, drink a green smoothie. For lunch, have some rice and some steamed vegetables. For dinner, only drink warm goat's milk. Do that for four months, and then we'll talk. If you can do that for four months, we'll send you to a panchakarma clinic in India where you'll spend one month getting a total cleanse. You'll get on a road to recovery, and you'll be fine."

I started following her prescriptions immediately, yet in the meantime, I had this thing going on in the background with this lieutenant colonel. I took a month off work to go to the panchakarma clinic where I disconnected myself from everybody. I did yoga, ate herbs, and got cleansed. I felt fantastic, and lost 30 lb. When I eventually had another MRI, one of those carotid arteries was clear, and blood was again flowing to the right side of my brain.

So I didn't die, yet by that time the lieutenant colonel had worked with us for a year, collecting an excellent salary of more than $150,000 plus stock options and other perks. By the end of the second year, I had been declared healthy. He didn't talk to me for the last six months of his employment. When it came time for his contract renewal, I renewed his contract with a slight increase.

When I gave it to him, he looked at me and said, "I can't renew my contract with you."

When I asked why not, he said, "You are an insult to the American way of life. You are an insult to the American government. Moreover, you are an insult to me personally."

"I'm sorry you feel that way," I said.

"I can't work for you," he said. "Either you get out of the company, or I'm not staying."

"I'm not leaving the company just because you don't get along with me. That's crazy. I don't know what you think you're here to do, but you're here to take over my position," I said.

"I know that. However, you never left."

I felt I couldn't leave, though, as I couldn't leave my company in the hands of this person I knew wasn't buying into our culture. I assumed he would come around, but I couldn't wait to see if he did. Incidentally, he never did come around. The power that people have is much more important than the force that countries have. One man with wisdom can change the course of a nation. Look at Gandhi, Jefferson or Martin Luther King. They didn't use guns; they had the power inside them.

David Hawkins is known as the father of behavioral kinesiology. For decades, he studied all the different methods that he could use on a person's body to react to simple "Yes" / "No" questions. He discovered that if you raise both your arms and someone pushes down on your hands, when you say, "All men are created equal," your arms become strong. If you say, "All men are created different and with varying levels of equality," your arms become weak.

Hawkins's theory is that behavioral kinesiology discovers the truth that your body feels through the input of energy that is spoken in words. He proved it in his books that you can rate all of the philosophies and ideas, whether they're economical, medical, philosophical or even religious, on a spectrum of enlightenment to force. He was a skilled and educated man, and if you read his books, and take them at face value, they would be a life-changing experience.

I gave Hawkins's book, *Power vs. Force*, to the lieutenant colonel and he threw it right out after randomly looking at five words and pronouncing it nonsense. There was no way to communicate to him that there was an alternative way to get things done that was an excellent way, a positive way and a good way that would help everybody. It would make a win-win situation instead of a win-lose situation for everybody.

The lieutenant colonel felt, however, that somebody had to be the dominant player and boss everybody else around. I couldn't communicate the benefit of positivity to him. When he left, he said, "You're a disgrace to the American government, and they shouldn't be giving you a single penny." I had wanted to renew his contract because I never give up on him. Every human being is a beautiful, incredible miracle that goes beyond explanation. Every human being — if you believe anything about behavioral kinesiology — has the truth residing inside of them like an incredible computer that's linked to every other human being and every other thing in the cosmos. We're all connected.

If all he had to do were remember that and connect to that, he would have been fine with us, and perhaps learned/remembered some things. I consider the lieutenant colonel's story a good result despite — or because of — the process. Everybody grew from it and moved forward and saw the value in an alternative way. They were witness to the stark contrast between the way that most organizations function and the way we function. I think it was to everybody's advantage to realize that some people are going to say, "I don't want this." They're going to reject it if they feel it's too counterintuitive and against everything they believe.

I listened to the lieutenant colonel, and I heard what he had to say. I didn't fire him, and I never told him to leave. There were times when I felt pretty bad about the situation, and about how bad I was failing, but I never fought it. I just went along with it. The beauty about this story was that everybody on the team was a witness to how this went down. The more trouble that happened with the lieutenant colonel, the more our people saw the value in the eight points, and the more they practiced them. They started to take the eight points more seriously. They began to hold meetings and talk to each other and share ideas about the concepts, organically growing the culture among themselves. The more that that happened, the angrier the lieutenant colonel became. Eventually, he couldn't stand being around any of us, and he left. So that was okay. The last words the lieutenant colonel spoke to me were, "You are wrong, and I am right."

As I've reiterated throughout this journey you've just taken with me, success and failure are both parts of the same sausage. With the lieutenant colonel, I did my best to turn our experience into a success, but you could say I failed. Alternatively, you could say his entire experience with us was a resounding success. His time at our company showed the rest of the team how vital these eight principles were to the success of our organization. With every fight he put up to dispel the potential success of our eight points, the rest of our people embraced them even more tightly.

If that's success, I'll take it.

CHAPTER NINE

WHERE DO WE GO FROM HERE?

Most of us don't really think about the past as we boldly trudge through the day. Chris Catranis seems to embrace the past, because its lessons are shaping his future. — Paul Gallagher, *Success*, Vol. 47 No. 4 (September 2000)

I hope you've embraced learning about the unusual or non-traditional ways in which I have done and continue to do business. While I've skipped around specific events in my life and the iterations of my business endeavors to illustrate the eight principles, I'm sure you can see that my path hasn't been straight, no matter how I tell the stories. As I conclude the book, I'd like to repeat what I said in the introduction. Given my somewhat unorthodox life experience, if I can adapt these eight principles to create a successful business path, anyone can.

My intention was not to write an inspirational book. Although I do want to encourage anybody in any possible way, shape or form, I want to do so by illustrating that you can see that despite my many challenges, if I can make my life turn out the way it's turned out by following these eight principles, anybody can. My story is one of inspiration in reverse. Some of my experiences have been so unattractive that just about anybody can apply the eight principles to their every-day life and become an astounding success.

My resume wouldn't exactly be called a standard blueprint for most leaders. Yet now that you've read my stories and disruptive screw-ups and successes, you can believe that in combining these eight principles with a graveyard spin you can come out on top. Hopefully, now that you know a bit about my path, you can now consider the possibilities that can happen when you combine your brand of creativity with your passion. For each of us, naturally, the combinations of the two will create a variety of different experiences and results.

The principles I've used to guide my personal and professional life

- ❖ Permit people to trust their own intuition and wisdom.

- ❖ Give people only as much information as they can handle.

- ❖ Don't take their power away. When we take decision-making power out of people's hands, we leave them feeling useless and incompetent.

- ❖ Keep your own ego out of it.

- ❖ Make them feel safe enough to fail.

- ❖ Give guidance and help with humility and thoughtfulness.

- ❖ Create a container for complex emotions, such as fear and trauma.

❖ Allow people to make different decisions and to have experiences that are different from what you expect.

Has the path I've taken worked perfectly every time? I'll let you be the judge. No matter how rocky or smooth my road has been, that's the path that life gave me, so it's the perfect path. Sometimes it's all in the way that you look back at the past. I happen to have the habit that when I look back, I search for the positive. Looking backward might be exciting or even enthusiastically wonderful, but at the very least it will be acceptable, as I am willing to accept what life brings me when I follow the eight principles. In looking back, you can see how it all fits together to become a source of peace and growth. The whole universe conspires to assist you in everything you do when you listen to your inner voice, as I learned in that Lebanese prison.

You can climb out of any circumstance in which you find yourself. Does the question become whether you're climbing out in the best way? On the cover of this book, you'll see a series of ladders — as I have great faith that any one of us can transcend our circumstances. All the ladders on the cover of the book are symbols of the thousands of ladders of the primary categories we all face — power, money, fame and pleasure. All are based on the same thing, which is that in seeking, we do not find.

At the bottom of my lowest ladder — when I was in jail in Lebanon — my inner voice finally found me in a state of silence, and it spoke up. I'd been asking for God to help me. I'd been asking my inner voice to help me. Of course, I didn't expect to be told, "Clean the toilet." I did, however, do that, and even though I didn't know it yet, it was at that point that I started to ascend the ladder.

There are many different derivations of those four ladders which people use to climb out of whatever circumstances they're seeking to transcend. The key, however, is to climb up the same ladder you climbed down on; that ladder you descended when you forgot about your inner voice, listened to your ego, and ended up at the bottom, feeling like a victim.

The only way out is going up the same ladder you climbed down. Perhaps the circumstance that you're in is fine, as it's in the acceptance of those circumstances where you find peace. If you're sad and you don't mind being sad, what happens to your sadness? It goes away. If you're unhappy and you don't mind being unhappy, what happens to your unhappiness? It goes away. Because the only thing that feeds those things and makes them worse is to complain about them and deny them. That happens from the ego; it doesn't happen from your inner voice.

Your inner voice will tell you that you brought yourself here, and ask what you're going to do. If you find yourself in this situation, ask your inner voice to show you the obstacles that are blocking you. Once you look at them, they start to dissolve. That's my ladder, and that's the ladder that appears when you give people space rather than opinions and theologies. There is only one ladder that we crawl down, but there are multiple fake ladders that we try to climb back up.

Once you regain power over your life and listen to your inner voice, you can live a life that's kind and gracious rather than one of scarcity and fear. Everybody can climb out of any set of circumstances, but the only way that you discover that ability is to realize that you have the ability. That comes from listening to your inner voice telling you what's blocking you from knowing you have the talent. Stop resisting your circumstances, accept them, and then you can move on up the very ladder you climbed down.

Give yourself much space just as you would give other people space. You don't have to choose to see things as terrible or wonderful, but rather see your experiences as lessons that we're all experiencing in this large classroom of life. All these self-made ladders of suffering are solutions that our ego is telling us we should take. They don't come from the inner voice. The key is to listen and find your heart and inner voice. When you follow these eight principles for others, you follow the same for yourself. It doesn't start with doing it with the outside; it starts from the inside.

Some people can meditate and hear their inner voice. Some do yoga and hear their inner voice. Some people can pray and hear their inner voice. Not everybody has to get hit over the head with a 2X4 to find their inner voice; it's encouraging to know that there's a path to go about this which is not painful. There's a way to your inner voice that does not have to involve all these things that have happened to me in my life. If you allow yourself to feel empathetic with yourself and others, strive to be a better listener, and watch for a little bit more insight, the type of transformation I'm talking about can happen for you.

The inner voice is one of love, and the eight principles are ways of expressing love in practical ways that lead to goodness and abundance. They point to an abundance in life in every direction as opposed to the scarcity you can experience when you're feeling afraid and being competitive, manipulative and controlling as we are often trained to be through our existing systems. These systems make us into various cogs in a big machine wanting to be a more and more critical cog in that machine. This machine revolves around fear and domination and exploitation and other harmful and toxic things.

There's nothing that demonstrates this gigantic machine of fear better in my mind than fossil fuels. The balloon on the cover of the book isn't a helium balloon; it's a hydrogen balloon, and is meant to illustrate my interest in using hydrogen as a clean source of energy. You could call this my next endeavor; that next toilet I want to clean. The last toilet to clean is the environment as I'd like to see the world rid of fossil fuels.

Imagine a word that isn't dependent on fossil fuel.

Imagine…
- no pollution;
- no energy companies;
- no political action committees of oil companies;
- no wars about oil;
- no poisons in our air, water and food;
- no young men going crazy from being poisoned, and shooting up schools;
- no slavery to paying energy bills;

- no petrodollars;
- a complete collapse of the oil-based world economy;
- no more toxic waste.

Then imagine a new era of human life.

In Chapter 33 of Jules Verne's book, *The Mysterious Island* (1874), a fascinating dialogue takes place:

"Oh! the veins of coal are still considerable, and the hundred thousand who annually extract from them a hundred millions of hundredweights have not nearly exhausted them."

"With the increasing consumption of coal," replied Gideon Spilett, "it can be foreseen that the hundred thousand workmen will soon become two

hundred thousand, and that the rate of extraction will be doubled."

"Doubtless; but after the European mines, which will be soon worked more

thoroughly with new machines, the American and Australian mines will for a

long time yet provide for the consumption in trade."

"For how long a time?" asked the reporter.

"For at least two hundred and fifty or three hundred years."

"That is reassuring for us, but a bad look-out for our great-grandchildren!" observed Pencroft.

"They will discover something else," said Herbert.

"It is to be hoped so," answered Spilett, "for without coal there would be

no machinery, and without machinery there would be no railways, no steamers, no manufactories, nothing of that which is indispensable to

modern civilization!"

"But what will they find?" asked Pencroft. "Can you guess, captain?"

"Nearly, my friend."

"And what will they burn instead of coal?" "Water," replied Harding.

"Water!" cried Pencroft, "water as fuel for steamers and engines! water to heat water!"

"Yes, but water decomposed into its primitive elements," replied Cyrus

Harding, "and decomposed doubtless, by electricity, which will then have

become a powerful and manageable force, for all great discoveries, by some

inexplicable laws, appear to agree and become complete at the same time.

Yes, my friends, I believe that water will one day be employed as fuel,

that hydrogen and oxygen which constitute it, used singly or together, will

furnish an inexhaustible source of heat and light, of an intensity of which

coal is not capable. Someday the coal rooms of steamers and the tenders of

locomotives will, instead of coal, be stored with these two condensed

gases, which will burn in the furnaces with enormous

calorific power. There
is, therefore, nothing to fear. As long as the earth is inhabited, it will
supply the wants of its inhabitants, and there will be no want of either
light or heat as long as the productions of the vegetable, mineral or
animal kingdoms do not fail us. I believe, then, that when the deposits of
coal are exhausted, we shall heat and warm ourselves with water. Water will
be the coal of the future."
"I should like to see that," observed the sailor.

Why is this snippet included in the conclusion? Because hydrogen is the energy source of the future, and I'm focused on making that happen. Water is just two parts hydrogen and one part oxygen. The technology to use hydrogen as a power source has been around for a long time, and it's completely doable.

Throughout this book, we've focused on the management principles more than the technology and the corporate strategy, but the initial framework is the same. The fact that I am what I would very humbly call a "disruptive leader" has naturally led to my love for and a firm embrace of disruptive technology. When I started USABROAD in 1979, it was by using disruptive technology to develop water systems for the Africans. That was the original vision of USABROAD.

What do I mean by disruptive technology now? In particular, I'm seeking to create positive social impact, and I'm introducing a way to use government programs to fund it — the EB-5 investor immigration program. The EB-5 program is the way to fund the vision. It's creative and has a better ROI than any existing company in the EB-5 industry. My hydrogen vision and EB-5 finance are the outworking of my entire career to date. They embody a theology of the ladder of environmental ascent. To learn more about the hydrogen vision of our project called Ascension City, please visit www.usabroad.net.

It may sound simple, but it's relevant for every one of us. We need to find our toilet to clean. That happens by following the eight principles up the very ladder you have climbed down, one rung at a time, step by step. Remember that the universe is always conspiring to help you live a fruitful life that benefits others. We can help each other win. It doesn't matter if it's in business or relationships; together, we can have a wonderful life experience.

BIBLIOGRAPHY

In addition to the following published sources, I recognize how Dr. Ronald Kavanaugh, my university professor, ignited my interest in the environmental crisis in a course called *Theology and the Environmental Crisis.*

Becker, Ernest, *The Denial of Death.* New York, 1973

Elder, Frederick Milton, *Crisis in Eden: a religious study of man and environment.* Nashville, 1970

Hawkins, David, *Letting Go: the pathway of surrender.* Carlsbad, 2013

   Power vs. Force: the hidden determinants of human behavior. Carlsbad, 2014

Plett, Heather, "What It Means to Hold Space for People, Plus Eight Tips on How to Do It Well." https://heatherplett.com/2015/03/hold-space/, posted on March 11, 2015, accessed on March 6, 2019

Schaeffer, Francis A., *Escape from Reason.* Chicago, 1968

   The God Who Is There. Chicago, 1968

   He Is There and He Is Not Silent. Wheaton, Il., 1972

Schucman, Helen, *A Course in Miracles.* New York, 1976

Tolle, Eckhart, *A New Earth: awakening to your life's purpose.* New York, 2005

Do you want to partner with Chris?

Go to www.chriscatranis.com
and find out how you can get involved in
Chris's next project!

42624139R00099

Made in the USA
Middletown, DE
16 April 2019